GENERATIONS OF PRIDE
A CENTENNIAL HISTORY OF INTERNATIONAL PAPER

The staff of the International Paper Centennial Book
Project would like to extend grateful appreciation to the
many employees, past and present, who have contributed
their time, artifacts and documents, and memories. We
are especially grateful to the people who participated in
oral history interviews in the United States and abroad,
and to the people who called the IP Centennial Phone
Line to record their reminiscences and anecdotes. Taken
as a whole, the artifacts, documents and memories of IP
employees constitute an unparalleled stockpile of information about the first century of International Paper's operations. These materials will serve as a significant resource
not only for the company's centennial, but for future IP
anniversaries.

CONTENTS

2   Foreword

6   *Generations of Pride* Stories

112   A Short History of International Paper

152   100 Years of Working for
      International Paper

156   International Paper from A to Z

A little more than 100 years ago, on January 31, 1898 to be exact, 17 pulp and paper mills in the northeastern United States joined to form the International Paper Company. Instantly, the new company's size, diversity of operations, quality of employees and community responsibility made it an industry leader. Remarkably, through the incredible evolution that defined the next 10 decades, from the automobile to the moon lander; from hand-cranked to cellular telephones; from the agricultural society to the global village, these attributes never changed. They still describe International Paper today, and more than that, they continue to be our company's greatest source of strength and its best hope for the next century.

FROM CUSHMAN RIDGE
LOOKING WEST
FOG IN VALLEYS
10 23 19

International Paper will be a global leader and provide an excellent financial return. We will be the company of choice for customers, shareholders, employees and suppliers, and we will be responsible members of the communities where we live and work. Ethical behavior and personal integrity are the core of our culture. With customers and facilities around the globe, we answer to the world.

These attributes are thoughtfully on display throughout this book, expressed by very talented and engaging authors who more than adequately represent the men and women who helped build International Paper.

You will read about legendary IP people, beginning with Hugh Chisolm, the man who served as president of our company in 1898. (The title of chief executive officer that we know today did not come about in the company until 1954.) Many other business leaders also truly earned the title of pioneer and are included in the personal stories that comprise the first section of our book. One of the dilemmas of all storytellers is the impossibility of mentioning all names that ought to be mentioned, so the names you will read here represent, and are in tribute to, a broader deserving population. Many of these people might not recognize our company's structure today —

they would be amazed at how teamwork, technology and the international marketplace, for instance, have changed our operations over the years. But they would easily recognize the roots of our strength in the Southern Kraft and Northern Divisions, the sales and marketing divisions, and the research facilities that they labored to create. The values of hard work, innovation, dedication to excellence and community and environmental partnerships have not changed at all.

This book was created by employees and retirees from around the world. From Jay, Maine to Natchez, Mississippi; from Corinth, New York to Gardiner, Oregon; from Ireland to New Zealand — and from

many more places in between. These employees provided recollections, anecdotes and stories about what it meant to be a part of a great company. I hope that by reading this book you will each have a deeper appreciation of the enormously rich heritage that our company is built upon.

In 1948, International Paper published a 50th Anniversary book. Like our current employees, the employees of that time believed they were a part of the best paper company in the world. I've been around International Paper long enough to have had the privilege of knowing — and learning from — many of these people. This book is dedicated to the hundreds of thousands of our employees and their families — past and present — who turned an 1890's dream into a better quality of life for many

generations and who have provided, as well, the inspiration

for a new century of even greater achievement.

And to those upon whom will fall the challenge of a

new century — a special note — this book is for you, too.

We are proud of what we have achieved in 100 years, and

we encourage you to expand the quest of continuous

improvement in serving the best interests of our customers,

shareowners, employees and communities.

John T. Dillon

GENERATIONS
OF
PRIDE

GENERATIONS OF PRIDE

Multiple generations of employees are common within International Paper. The McCarthy family — Sue, Kevin and Matthew (foreground) — are examples. Sue's father, Romeo St. Pierre (wearing hat) had a career of nearly 40 years at the Otis and Androscoggin mills in Maine. Sue and Kevin both began working in the Land & Timber Department which had offices in the mill. They now work in the Northeast Region-Land & Timber and each has more than 20 years with the company. Matthew became the star of two nationwide International Paper TV commercials. Both of Matthew's great grandfathers — Francis Moreau and Xavier Goulet (center in portrait) — have company roots that go nearly to International Paper's beginnings.

A NOTE TO THE READER The following anecdotes are from current and former employees of International Paper worldwide, through oral history interviews, recorded stories from the IP Centennial Phone Line, and published and unpublished reminiscences. In some cases, where appropriate, an anecdote has been edited for context and clarity. Where an anecdote was provided in a language other than English, both the original version and a translation appear. Unless noted otherwise, the date of an anecdote is 1997.

One of the biggest things we as foresters have not impressed people enough with is the *renewability* of the resource. Forestry *is renewal*. Even if we don't do anything out there, the forest is going to grow something. It's not like coal, which is extractable and when it's gone, it's gone. The forest you can regenerate. And we've *done it*. The paper industry helped develop what became known as the "Second Forest." IP played a major role in that whole thing, and it ended up that we did a pretty good job, because somewhere toward the late 1950s or early 1960s we were growing more timber than we were cutting across the South. Now we're talking about the "Third Forest"—the whole genetic story and all that sort of thing.

Kendall Dexter, interview, Mobile, Alabama.

Part of the "Second Forest," near Natchez, Mississippi.

Credit: Courtesy Lillie E. DeShields, Natchez mill.

Papyrus, a paper-like
material, developed in
ancient Egypt.

Paper produced in ancient
China by Ts'ai Lun.

First known paper made
from rags invented in China.

3000 BC   105 AD   150

What I really see more than anything is that IP is a lot like
America in general. I see hard work, dedication, traditional
values, and if you adhere to those rules, you can climb the
ladder. I've met people along the way who've made it—there
are success stories throughout the mill, throughout the company.
It all goes back to the things that built America. And just like
America, International Paper continues to evolve, to develop.

That's what I see the company continuing to do. As long as we
stay on the track of hard work, values, keeping ourselves in the
right direction, striving forward, trying to do the things we say
we're going to do, being high quality, then this company is going
to be around for a long time. A lot of good people are going to
be a part of it. We're going to continue to have great experiences
for the next 100 years, and I hope I'm a part of it for as long
as I can be.

Kirk Clayborn, interview, Texarkana mill, Texarkana, Texas.

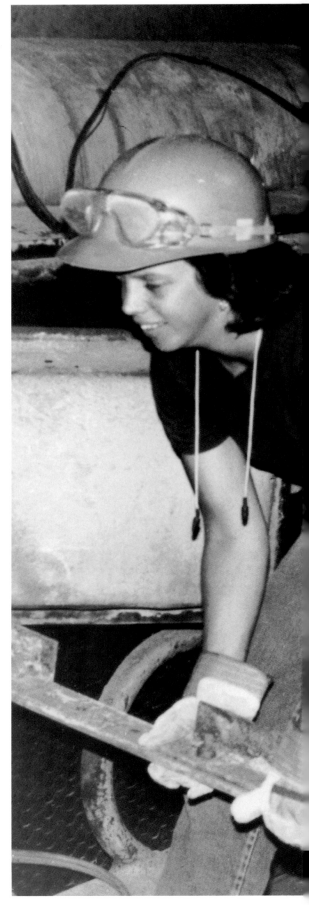

First European paper mill built at Fabriano, Italy.

Quirl paper mill built, later acquired by Zanders Feinpapiere AG, Germany, later an IP subsidiary.

Kiesenbrodt's Gut paper mill built, later acquired by Zanders Feinpapiere AG, Germany, later an IP subsidiary.

1268   1582   1602   ▶▶→

Maintenance crew at Louisiana mill, Bastrop, Louisiana.

Credit: Courtesy Kinny Haddox, Louisiana mill.

Upper Dombach mill built, later acquired by Zanders Feinpapiere AG,Germany, later an IP subsidiary.

First paper made in the United States by William Rittenhouse, Germantown, Pennsylvania.

Lower Dombach mill built, later acquired by Zanders Feinpapiere AG, Germany, later an IP subsidiary.

1614   1690   1699   ⟫→

Back then in the 1940s and 1950s, most of the black fellows worked as laborers in the "bull gang." I remember when a job came up for bid for a combination helper (a worker who monitors the process) on the recovery boiler in the Power Plant, and I wanted it. Everybody told me, "A black man won't get that kind of job." I told the white foreman that I wanted that job and had as much right to it as any white man. Everyone got real quiet and a lot of my black friends told me I'd messed up. But the next day, it was posted that I had that job.

I was the first black man in this mill to get a job like that, and I got it because I spoke up.

J. T. Roberson, interview, Moss Point mill, Mississippi.

J. T. Roberson checks de-mister on the No. 3 Recovery Boiler dissolving tank vent stack, Moss Point mill.

J. T. Roberson, 1997.

Frenchman Louis Robert
invented and patented
the Fourdrinier machine.

Frenchman Alexis
Aussedat took control
of a paper mill in Crane
that later became central
production facility of
Aussedat Rey, later an
IP subsidiary.

Formation of J. W.
Zanders, predecessor of
Zanders Feinpapiere
AG, Germany, later an
IP subsidiary.

1799   **1806**   **1829**

Veronica O'Donnell

Credit: Courtesy Nancy Hillis,
Purchase, New York.

Mechanical or ground-wood pulp process patented by Friedrich G. Keller in Germany. Patent later sold to Heinrich Völter, who improved process.

William Beckett and associates started Beckett newsprint mill in Hamilton, Ohio.

Coated papers introduced in the United States.

1844   1848   1852 ⟫→

We're all trained on different machines on the line that actually makes the panel

doors. We are all multi-skilled on the machines so we can swap around so it

doesn't get boring. We still have ongoing training, so that keeps it interesting.

Everybody seems to be in good form. They have the work organized in such a

way that you're really involved. They leave it up to you if something goes wrong

with the machine. You know best—you've been working on it—so you, along

with a maintenance person, make a decision about what should be done, or the

fastest way to get the machine going again.

Masonite Ireland has employed an awful lot of people that were out of work

in the area here, and it brought back a lot of people who were away. They

came home and got jobs—it was something steady for them to come back to.

It's a well-based company and it has a good future, so people were happy to

see it come.

Veronica O'Donnell, Masonite Ireland, interview.

Children of mill employees deliver lunches to the Otis mill in Livermore Falls, Maine, in these photographs originally published in the November 1963 issue of The Otis News. Clockwise, from the top left: Laurence Chicoine, Jr.; Angela Castonguay, daughter of Bert Castonguay; Mike Luciano, son of Tony Luciano; and Michelle Hennessey, daughter of Conrad and granddaughter of Anatole Hennessey.

Credit: Courtesy Don LeClerc, Wausau Papers, Livermore Falls, Maine.

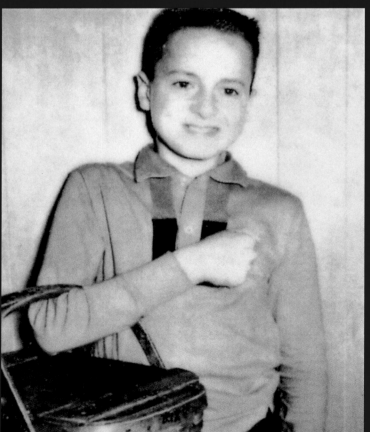

I have many childhood memories of taking my Dad's hot lunch to him while he was working at the Otis mill's steam plant in Livermore Falls, Maine, on Saturdays or in the summer when I was not in school. Sometimes I'd just leave his dinner, but more often I'd sit down on the bench with him as he ate his meal, with my mouth watering, since I hadn't yet had my lunch. Sometimes he'd give me a taste of his delicious dinner, which my Mother, Helen (a superb cook), had prepared.

Carolyn Bean Merchant, "Otis Memories from Gerald Bean's Daughter."

Western Newspaper Union formed in Omaha, Nebraska, later part of IP's distribution business.

Construction of Hudson River mill at Corinth, New York, by Albrecht and Alberto Pagenstecher and associates; Hudson River later became one of IP's 17 original mills.

Rey Company, a major French tannin producer, founded; later merged with Aussedat Paper Company to form Aussedat Rey, later an IP subsidiary.

1865   1869   1871   ⟫→

Papermaking is more of a science than an art today, naturally, with all the equipment that you've got and everything. But by the same token, to me—and probably I still got my foot in a rut—I would still like to be able to have a mixture of both things, where the guy learns the art part as well as the science part—then he'd be a complete person, a complete papermaker. There are still some things that you need to pay attention to that the science has not caught up with. You're relying on instruments, you know.

I've gone out on the floor a lot of times and I've said to the guy who's running the machine, "What's going on out here today?"

"Whadya mean, 'what's going on'?"

A worker observes as corrugated board is pasted onto a liner, Georgetown container plant, Georgetown, South Carolina, circa 1946.

Credit: Courtesy Lois Markstrom, Corporate Secretary's Office, Purchase, New York.

I said, "I can feel vibrations in the floor that I didn't feel here before." I said, "You've got a problem in here someplace." And we'd start looking around and we'd find that there was a bearing that was going, or something that was going on that didn't show up on any instrumentation or any computers or anything at that time.

See, those are a lot of the things that the older people—who came up without that stuff, in the art form—get used to looking for and feeling. They've got all those senses of feeling, and listening to different noises, and that stuff. They knew when things were going the way they should be and when they were not, because they paid attention to them. Today, everybody's looking at the video monitor to get all their information—they don't go around the machine and listen to it.

George White, interview, Androscoggin mill, Jay, Maine.

Corrugated medium patented in the United States.

Formation of R. A. Long Company, a lumber yard in Columbus, Kansas, later reorganized into Long-Bell Lumber Corporation, a former IP subsidiary.

Formation of Friedenwald Company, later renamed Lord Baltimore Press, an IP subsidiary.

Construction of Ticonderoga, New York, mill, later acquired by IP, known as Lower Falls mill.

1871   **1875**   **1878**

In 1947, I joined Single Service Containers, Inc., then a subsidiary of IP and later its Single Service Division. The name "single service" meant that the containers were used only once rather than returned for use like glass bottles. In 1949, I became sales service manager for the division's Bastrop territory, which covered all of the South, East to the Carolinas, North to Minnesota, West to Washington and the West Coast, and all states in between—plus Mexico and Venezuela. Most shipments were rail carload.

In the early formative years our plants progressed from the original three—Bastrop, Louisiana; Kalamazoo, Michigan; and Norristown, Pennsylvania—to 16 across the United States by the mid-1960s. During this period, glass bottles were rapidly being replaced by paper containers. The impact of plastic to our market was formidable. It forced us to look at expanding and diversifying our market, which resulted in IP moving heavily into juice markets, plus overseas expansion—Japan, Korea, and Taiwan.

Richard R. Hornbeak, reminiscences.

Invention of the folding
carton.

Lock Haven, Pennsylvania,
mill built, later acquired
by IP.

Invention of sulfate pulp
process.

Staff of the Single Service Division's plant in Miami, Florida, 1965. The division operated 16 other plants throughout the United States during the 1960s.

Credit: Courtesy Charles R. Slater, Seminole, Florida.

Lake George Paper
Company built plant in
Ticonderoga, New York,
known as the Island mill,
later one of IP's 17
original mills.

Horace Moses started
construction of Strathmore
mill at Mittineague,
Massachusetts, later
acquired by IP.

Seventeen pulp and paper
mills merged to form
International Paper.

1891   **1892**   **1898**

*Products bearing the Hammermill
brand name are used in offices
around the world.*

Credit: Courtesy Investor Relations,
Purchase, New York.

IP elected Hugh Chisholm
president.

Hammermill Paper
Company founded in
Erie, Pennsylvania.

IP issued its first annual
report.

1898   1899

*Maintenance crew, Louisiana mill,
Bastrop, Louisiana.*

Credit: Courtesy Kinny Haddox,
Louisiana mill, Bastrop, Louisiana.

OVERLEAF

*The Masonite Ireland facility in
Carrick-on-Shannon, Republic of
Ireland, began operations in 1996.*

Credit: Courtesy Mary Cullen,
Masonite Ireland.

American Realty Company, an IP woodlands subsidiary, incorporated in Maine.

IP started Central Test Bureau at Glens Falls, New York, the first laboratory in the American pulp and paper industry.

IP issued instructions forbidding the cutting of trees below a certain size.

IP organized Champlain Realty Company, New York, a woodlands subsidiary.

Formation of Transo Envelope Company, later renamed Avery Corporation, later part of IP's distribution business.

1901   1904

Our people work very well together. They know what the competition is, who it is, and what they have to do to beat it. They give a good day's work, and you can bet that if there's a way to do their job a little better, they'll find it.

Cecil O. Bailey, Jr., quoted in "Production Thrives in Historic Vicksburg Setting," *The International Paper*, May-June 1984, p. 8.

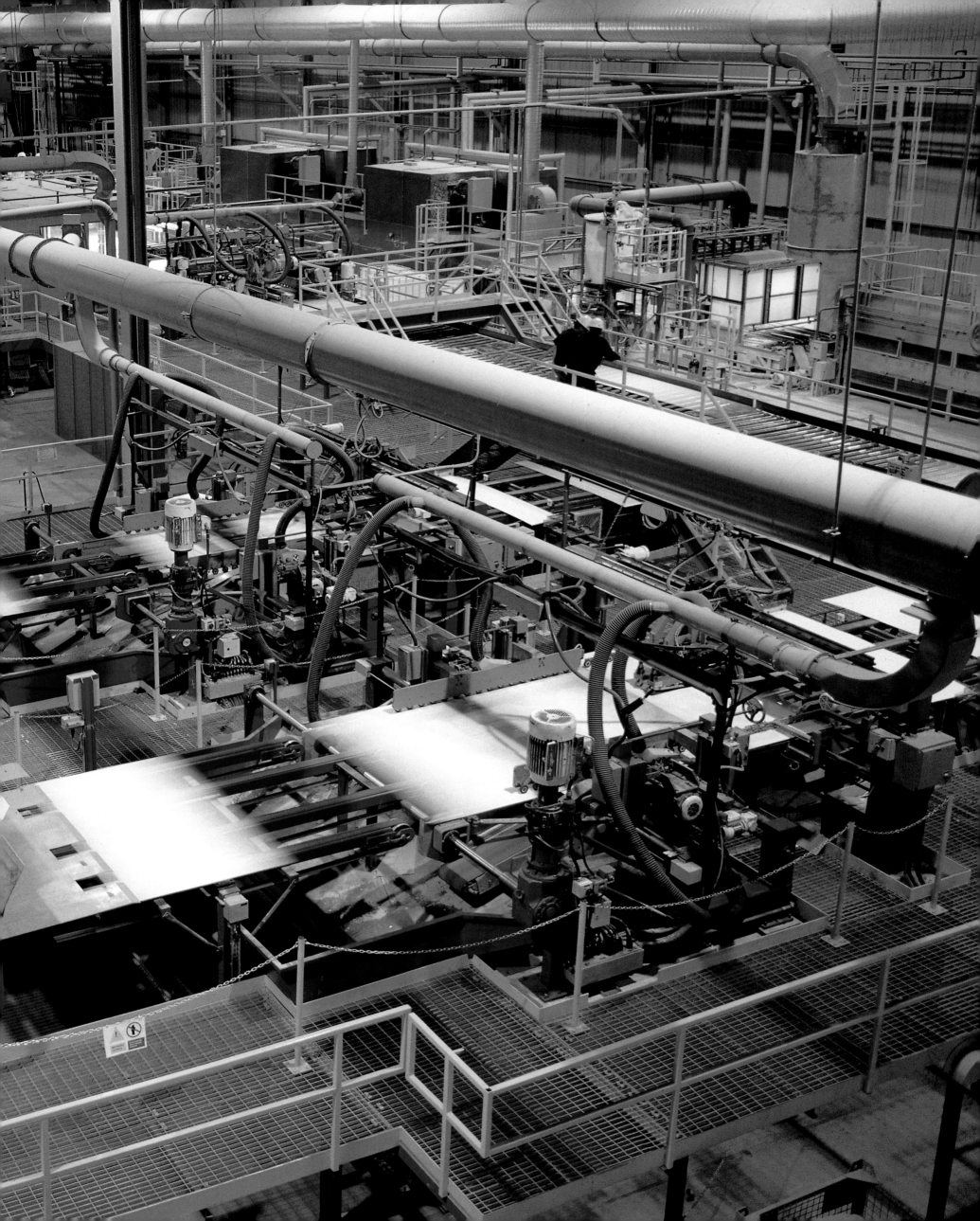

A pickaroon is like an ax only it's pointed on the end instead of a blade. You just reached out and hooked a piece of wood and pulled it to wherever you wanted it.

You could either stab it and pull it through, or you could hook it and pull it to where you want it to go.

Mac McLean, interview, Augusta, Maine.

PICKAROON

*This pickaroon was used by
Lawrence Bledsloe, a crane operator
in the woodyard at Hot Springs,
Arkansas. Using pickaroons,
Bledsloe and another employee
could unload a rail car of wood
in five minutes.*

Credit: Courtesy Lawrence Bledsloe,
Arkadelphia, Arkansas.

*Workers loading pulpwood onto
conveyor, Georgetown mill,
circa 1946.*

Credit: Courtesy Corporate Archives,
Purchase, New York.

Horace Moses acquired Woronoco, Massachusetts, mill, later merged into Strathmore Paper Company, subsequently acquired by IP.

Hammermill Paper Company produced 60 private watermarks.

IP exported 36,198 tons of paper.

1904   1905

We're like a one-stop shopping center. This is why I consider myself lucky, being with *xpedx* rather than with a company that sells paper alone, or with a company that sells equipment alone, or possibly *supplies* alone. It's lucky, especially if you're on a commission basis, if you have that opportunity to work up a volume where you can sell all *three* of those lines. We've got paper, we've got printing equipment and we've got supplies. And as big as International Paper Company is, we've got *tremendous* lines, tremendous lines—I mean, *the best*. We've got a golden opportunity to put all this stuff together.

Joe Strauss, interview, Houston, Texas.

The regional distribution facility which xpedx *opened in 1995 in Dallas, Texas, is equipped to service customers using state-of-the-art inventory management technology.*

Credit: *International Paper Company Annual Report for 1995.*

IP introduced 8-hour, three-shift system in several trades.

Formation of the International Brotherhood of Pulp, Sulfite, and Paper Mill Workers.

A. Burbank elected IP President.

Construction of IP groundwood mill at Livermore Falls, Maine.

Business depression affected IP's sales.

1906   1907

My job as an accounts salesman had the best of both worlds—responsibility and diversity. One day I might be going over product strategy with the White Papers Group's senior marketing management, and that afternoon I could be down at the customer's production line troubleshooting a feeding problem with our technical reps. Tomorrow I might be writing an analysis of our competition for the product managers. Next week I could be spending a day with a fork lift operator figuring out some way to unload 40 rolls of paper jammed in a freight car a plant manager is threatening to send back to our mill. Good communication within IP and with our customers ranks high on my priority list. Basically, I get things done by using all our resources.

Bob Waltz (national accounts salesman, White Papers), quoted in "A Day on the road: Selling IP As Well as Its Products," *Viewpoints*, Summer 1980, p.10.

Handling merchants in New York City was always the area to go for someone who really wants to find out the operations of the paper business. Every day there is a new deal. For inside men, the training program was the job, and it was the best training program you could get. The *real* training was everyday life sitting down with the New York merchants—who are the toughest in the world.

Marty Murphy, interview, Rockville Centre, New York.

IP's board of directors voted to manage the company's timberlands and those of its subsidiaries according to latest forestry science.

IP customers included the following newspapers:

New York Times, 7,500 tons
Chicago Tribune, 15,000 tons
Chicago Daily News, 30,000 tons

Baltimore American, 5,000 tons
Springfield Republican, 800 tons
Providence Tribune, 1,800 tons
Providence Journal, 3,000 tons

IP's Champlain Realty Company started tree nursery in Vermont.

1908

Bob Waltz, National Accounts Salesman, White Papers Group, 1980.

Credit: *Viewpoints*, Summer 1980.

IP hired first mill nurse.

Sulfate pulp process introduced in the United States.

Strathmore and Woronoco mills merged to form Strathmore Paper Company.

Hammermill Paper Company doubled its production capacity to meet skyrocketing demand for fine paper.

Formation of Dixon Paper Company, later part of IP's distribution business.

1910   1911

The last 10 years I worked for International Paper—from 1975 to 1985 when I retired—I worked in the environmental area with the gaseous emissions problem. And that was a real challenge. I had to learn an awful lot of chemistry, an awful lot of mill processes and everything else. During that time, I went to every mill that the company owned, except the Hudson River mill. I worked in and out of Georgetown a good bit, Natchez a good bit, and then the various mills, and Mansfield with their start-up and operation. There was a chemical engineer who worked with me, and a couple of technicians. We spent a lot of time on the road, going around with our little van.

During that time, there was so much development of instrumentation in that area that nobody wanted to spend any money to buy any equipment—it was developing so fast, so they didn't want to invest what was a tremendous amount of money. But we helped them work out some of the details and helped solve some of the problems they were having, and tried to help them to learn some of the things we had learned. I really learned an awful lot, and I really enjoyed that— working in the mills and getting to know more about the mill processes and the recovery processes and all.

Metha Schlish, interview, Mobile, Alabama.

Hammermill developed innovative marketing plan for fine papers.

Underwood Tariff Act removed tariffs on newsprint. Imports from Canada increased, IP's northeastern U. S. newsprint mills suffered as a result.

IP's market share in United States newsprint was 26 percent.

Moss Point, Mississippi, mill started operations, one of the first mills to successfully utilize Southern pine.

Philip Dodge elected IP president.

The Mobile Emissions Research Laboratory (MERLAB) analyzed gaseous emissions at IP's manufacturing facilities.

Credit: Courtesy Corporate Research Center, International Paper (1984).

War in Europe affected
IP's export business as
freight rates increase.

IP operated 16 mills in
the United States with
0.5 million tons capacity.

IP eliminated its floating
debt.

IP dividends on preferred
stock, 2 percent for the
past eight years,
increased to 6 percent.

| 1914 | 1915 | 1916 |

In 1976, the company went through a major reorganization. That was the day

that they dismantled the Southern Kraft Division and Northern Division,

and took the mills and put them under the direction of what we called "Strategic

Business Unit Managers," who then were running both marketing and

manufacturing. They were full general managers, in effect.

It was quite a day, and I well remember it. Several hundred executives within the company all had new jobs thrust upon them in a single day. They marched all of us over to the Grand Ballroom in the Waldorf Astoria Hotel. Stan Smith was the chairman then, and he was something of a colorful man.

Government comman-
deered most steamships
and railroad cars used for
transportation to and
from IP mills. IP bought
railroad cars to avoid
transportation problems.

1917

He was on the stage, and he would call out a name and say, "Here's your new

assignment. That's what you're going to do." People's heads were turning in

some cases because they found themselves in jobs for which they weren't totally

ready or there was no background there that made it fit. But the people who

were masterminding the reorganization felt that they should be stretched into this

thing. It was quite remarkable, particularly the colorful way it was carried out.

It was a good reorganization. It needed to be done. If you were going to set up a

truly responsible management organization, it needed to control all of the aspects

of its business—and that included both manufacturing and marketing. It married

the customers' needs to the marketing organization and to the manufacturing

entity that could satisfy those needs by supplying the products that were needed.

Charles Connelly, interview, Memphis Operations Center, Memphis, Tennessee.

*Working draft of corporate
organization chart under the
reorganization of 1976.*

Credit: Courtesy Corporate Research
Center, Sterling Forest, New York.

IP improved its accident prevention program.

IP voluntarily increased wages.

Formation of Edgewater Paper Company in Menasha, Wisconsin, later renamed Akrosil, subsequently acquired by IP.

IP produced 305,708 tons of newsprint and 166,299 tons of other grades.

IP mills in Piercefield, New York; Bellows Falls, Vermont; and Franklin, New Hampshire, converted from newsprint to specialty papers. Conversion of Niagara Falls newsprint mill started.

1917 **1919** ⟫➤

In the late 1950s when the Mississippi was in flood, the make-up yard for the

Natchez mill was very near the river. During one of those waters we noticed

what we thought was a big dog over in the hay house. The next day it turned out

to be a black bear, escaping from the high water over in Louisiana. And one of

the stickmen decided that he would leave his lunch. He walked over toward the

hay house, put his dinner down, and then came back. Apparently the bear had

watched him from inside the door of the hay house, and as soon as we were

out of her sight and behind some racks watching, she came out and she ate

the lunch.

Flooded lands adjacent to the Natchez mill, 1973.

Credit: Courtesy Lillie E. DeShields, Natchez mill.

So we went by the cafeteria and we asked the cafeteria manager if he would save

the cut-offs for us. He said he would save them. So we picked 'em up and took

'em out, every day, and we fed the bear. She was always hungry, apparently, and

she would come out and get it almost before we would leave. And we decided

that we would name her. She was asking for the food, so we decided that we

would name her "Bear-Ask."

Henry Charles Doherty, recorded story, IP Centennial Phone Line.

"Boss"

"Get a weigh sheet"

Machine Room workers, Mobile mill, Mobile, Alabama, demonstrating hand signals, 1962.

Credit: Courtesy Mobile mill, *Panorama*, August 1962, and Karen Harris, Mobile mill.

"Hurry"

"Paper Break"

It's a pretty noisy environment in a paper mill. Back then, most of the communication was done by some kind of sign language. There were about 10 or 12 different signs and everybody on the paper machine under-stood them.

David Parks, interview, Georgetown, South Carolina.

IP acquired sulfate mill at Van Buren, Maine, to produce kraft pulp.

IP subsidiary started construction of a paper mill at Three Rivers, Quebec.

Hammermill Paper Company introduced innovative system of employee benefits, including paid vacations.

IP used more than 1,000 horses in the woods.

Richard Cullen and associates formed Bastrop Pulp and Paper Company, a pioneer in Southern kraft production.

1919 **1920** ⟫→

Longshoremen at a dock in Baton Rouge, Louisiana, load a shipment of pulp from the Natchez mill for shipment to Japan.

Credit: *International Paper Company Annual Report for 1989.*

I have been with International Paper Company (Japan) more than 22 years. I began as secretary to the vice-president, and for more than 12 years I have been sales coordinator for pulp sales. I send orders and coordinate shipping between customers and the mill. We have three mills in the U.S. that produce pulp for Japan—Natchez, Texarkana and Georgetown. From Texarkana we are selling fluff pulp for manufacturers of disposable diapers and incontinence products. We are selling fluff pulp and pine (softwood) pulp from Georgetown for diapers, wallpaper and bleached board. From Natchez, we are selling dissolving pulp as a raw material for film and plastics. We are a first-class supplier in Japan for pulp sales. We are selling more than 100,000 tons in Japan this year, and we service a very big volume in Japan.

I feel that IP is the very first-class paper company in the world. Working for this company is my pride. I like the atmosphere here, I have a good boss, the process is very good and the business is growing—this is why I have stayed for 22 years. Mr. Dillon's agenda for IP employees is very reasonable, very good, and I am trying to achieve it.

Mieko Kurihara, interview, Tokyo, Japan.

Formation of General
Crude Oil Company, later
acquired by IP.

IP's Three Rivers, Quebec,
mill started operations
with four paper machines.

IP's Niagara Falls, New
York, mill converted to
sulfite bond and book
papers.

IP's Employees' Mutual
Benefit Association
(EMBA) formed.

1922   **1923**

In 1965, a group of 12 newly hired young men did their sales

training down South in Mobile, Alabama. As future sales

managers in Europe, we could participate in a very thorough,

motivating and interesting U.S. training program before

returning to our office in Zurich, Switzerland.

Out of that group of 12, at least three are still with our

company: John T. Dillon, who, after joining our International

Pulp sales office in New York, went on to become our Chairman

and CEO; Hans Peter Daroczi, who now heads International

Container, and myself, Director Commercial for International

Paper Company (Europe). I think that, 32 years later, this is a

pretty good result for IP and for us—although one person from

the group will not be able to further improve his position with

the company . . . .

Nicholas A. Pult, reminiscences.

1923

One of the things that we have done after IP's acquisition of a majority interest in Carter Holt Harvey is that we are now sharing an office with Carter Holt (Japan). I'm particularly happy that we've been able to make that happen. The two companies complement each other very well. What has happened is that we have a presence in Japan, but in paper and pulp. In the United States, IP sells wood products, like 2 x 4's, Masonite, that type of thing. But we don't sell them in Japan because IP (Japan) doesn't have anyone who can sell wood products. Now, Carter Holt, their people are selling basically wood products—the 2 x 4's, the plywood, and that type of thing. They do have capability to sell IP's wood products—so we're discussing that possibility. On the other hand, Carter Holt produces pulp, containerboard and paper, but it does not have anybody who is selling paper in Japan. So we're also discussing the possibility of IP (Japan) selling some of the Carter Holt paper on their behalf. So I think there's potential help in both directions.

Fujio Hayashi, interview, Tokyo, Japan.

Archibald Graustein elected IP president.	Expansion of IP's Three Rivers, Quebec, newsprint mill, from four to seven machines, started.	Construction of Louisiana mill in Bastrop, Louisiana, started.		St. Maurice Lumber Company, a wholly owned subsidiary of IP, renamed Canadian International Paper Company.	IP acquired large interest in New England Power Association.

1924   **1925**

Akira Takita (l.), Mitsui Co., Ltd., and Keiji Kodo, senior vice president, Japan International Paper Company (Asia), review a bill of lading for a shipment of pulp sent from the United States to a warehouse in Yokohama City, 1975. In September 1994, JIPCO changed its name to International Paper Company (Japan), Ltd., to avoid confusion with IP's newly opened Asia sales office in Hong Kong.

Credit: Courtesy L.C. Sloan, Georgetown, South Carolina.

We had a very talented man by the name of Thomas Busch who for many years headed all of our mechanical logging research. He developed a lot of machinery that influenced later developments in logging manufacturing operations. The most famous of his inventions was the Busch Combine or "Buschmaster." It was a machine that took individual trees and harvested them, delimbed them, cut them in lengths, and put them in stacks. It was a labor-saving device that led to many others, such as the system of loading stacked wood onto barges with a gantry crane and a sling.

Many other pieces of equipment which are used today include parts of the machinery systems that Tom Busch developed at IP facilities.

Norman Gamso, interview, Mobile, Alabama.

Busch Combine in operation, circa 1960.

Credit: Courtesy Jack Williams, Mobile, Alabama.

IP acquired mill at
Ticonderoga, New York,
known as the Lower
Falls mill.

IP acquired Bastrop Pulp
and Paper Company with
sulfate kraft pulp and
paper mill at Bastrop,
Louisiana.

Canadian International
Paper started construc-
tion of newsprint mill at
Gatineau, Quebec.

Formation of Mason Fibre
Company, later renamed
Masonite Corporation, an
IP subsidiary.

1925

Loving Arms is an organization that is set up to provide emotional, financial and even spiritual support to women and infants with HIV/AIDS. I got involved with the group several years ago because I like babies, and I found out that this organization would allow you to go into the hospital in Memphis that cares for indigent people, and let you hold these babies and give them a little love and attention. No one wanted to hold them once they found out that the mother was HIV-positive. But I wanted them to remember that they'd had loving arms around them.

The Loving Arms organization was strictly volunteer—the head of the group was running it from her own house and didn't have a copier, a fax machine, anything like that. They were spending money running over to the copier store to get things copied or faxed. Imagine it's raining and you've got a client in there and you have to go three or four blocks to get something copied. That's why, after I began volunteering with them, I decided to approach the International Paper Company Foundation about their Volunteers of International Paper (VIP) grants. We got a $500 grant from the foundation, and used it to buy a combination fax machine, copier, printer and answering machine that was on sale for $499.

Loving Arms Zoo Day, 1997.

Credit: Courtesy Carolyn Daugherty, Memphis.

My chest was stuck out after that, of course. I really felt good knowing that it was my company doing this. It's concerned about the community, stretching its arms out to encompass all of the areas that surround where we have facilities. We're concerned about the world, we're concerned about people, we're concerned about these HIV-positive mothers and babies.

Carolyn Daugherty, interview, Memphis.

Canadian International
Paper's Three Rivers,
Quebec, mill completed
large-scale expansion and
became the world's
largest newsprint mill.

IP's Champlain Realty
Company with its nursery
in Randolph, Vermont,
planted 182,000 spruce
trees and 26,000 pine
trees as part of reforestation effort.

International Power and
Paper Company of
Newfoundland, Ltd.
formed by IP to acquire
large newsprint mill at
Corner Brook,
Newfoundland.

IP acquired Louisiana
Pulp and Paper Company
from Richard Cullen and
associates.

1926   **1927**   ≫→

*Students at an elementary school in
Mobile, Alabama, in 1973, improve
their oral communications skills
through a program supported by
the International Paper Company
Foundation.*

Credit: Courtesy Karen Harris,
Mobile mill.

Formation of Southern
International Paper
Company, wholly owned
subsidiary of IP, predeces-
sor of Southern Kraft
Division.

IP's Piercefield, New York,
mill converted to bond
paper.

Canadian International
Paper completed installa-
tion of a fire prevention
system at Gatineau,
Quebec.

IP acquired George &
Sherrard Paper Company
to manufacture multiwall
paper cement sacks. Later
became a major user of
Southern kraft paper.

IP started kraft mill in
Camden, Arkansas.

1927   **1928**

Over the years that I've been with the union, we've had some bad places in the road, but overall, I think we've had a pretty good relationship with the company. We can talk to each other about problems, if we have problems.

Billy Hipp, interview, Texarkana mill, Texarkana, Texas.

We in Industrial Relations had very good relations with the majority of our union representatives. We had a working relationship. We knew they had a job to do, they knew we had a job to do. And it was easier to solve a problem with some of them than it was with others. But we all tried to work together.

Lee Weeks, interview, Mobile, Alabama.

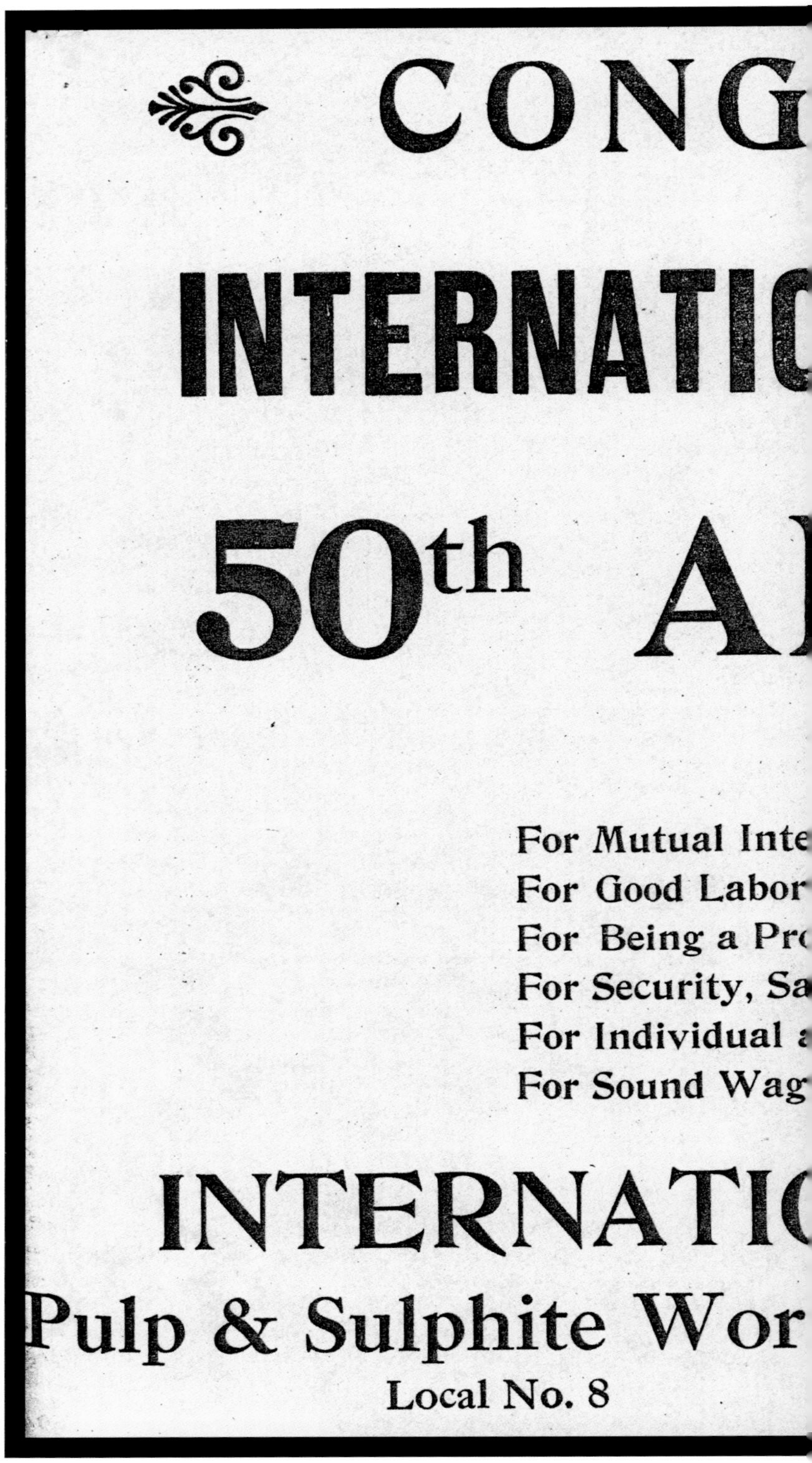

CONG
INTERNATIO
50th AI

For Mutual Inte
For Good Labor
For Being a Pro
For Security, Sa
For Individual a
For Sound Wag

INTERNATIO
Pulp & Sulphite Wor
Local No. 8

RATULATIONS

...TO...

NAL PAPER COMPANY

...ON...

NNIVERSARY

ITANY OF LABOR

of Employers and Employees===We give thee thanks
nagement Relations   ===We give thee thanks
sive Industry   ===We give thee thanks
and Welfare   ===We give thee thanks
Collective Cooperation   ===We give thee thanks
d Working Conditions   ===We give thee thanks

NAL BROTHERHOODS of

rs   Papermakers   Firemen & Oilers
Local No. 11   Local No. 247

Advertisement in Livermore Falls Advertiser, *June 10, 1948.*

Credit: Courtesy Corporate Archives, Purchase, New York.

IP acquired Moss Point,
Mississippi, mill together
with 45,600 acres of
timberlands.

Formation of International
Paper and Power Company
as a holding company for IP
and its hydroelectric power
business.

IP acquired 42,000 acres
of Southern timberland
for Mobile mill.

IP started kraft mill in
Mobile, Alabama.

1928   **1929**

I worked over 33 years for
International Paper Company at the
Niagara mill. But my association
started long before I was hired at the
mill. When I was a child growing up,
International in the early 1920s built
nearly 100 new homes for employees
on Shepard and Curtis Avenues in the
LaSalle section of Niagara Falls, a
block away from where I lived. These
streets were named in honor of the
President and Vice-President of

Dr. John Campbell named IP's first Director of Research.

Stock Market crash signaled the beginning of the Great Depression that affected the pulp and paper industry throughout the following decade.

Creditors' committee took control of Federal Paper Board Company, later merged with IP.

IP's Island mill in Ticonderoga, New York, closed.

Arizona Chemical formed as a joint venture of IP and American Cyanamid.

1930 ⫸→

International Paper at the time. When Piercefield mill shut down in the early 1930s, most of those people moved into this housing.

OVERLEAF
La Salle Housing Corporation Development, May 1924.

Credit: Courtesy Kevin McCarthy, Augusta, Maine.

I later became the paper boy for all these International Paper Company people. I came to know most of them, and got to know the personnel and the stories of the Niagara mill. So when I started work at International I was almost a veteran.

Roy Goodson, reminiscences.

IP closed Ticonderoga
(Upper Falls), New York
mill.

IP's Camden, Arkansas,
mill started multiwall
bag plant.

IP's Central Test Bureau at
Glens Falls, New York,
renamed Glens Falls
Research Laboratory.

Southern International
Paper Company, an IP
subsidiary, renamed
Southern Kraft
Corporation.

1930

On the 17th day of April, 1940, we left Phoenix for New York by way of Monroe, Louisiana; Atlanta; and we got as far as Richmond, Virginia. The weather was really bad, with icing conditions all the rest of the way. We had no de-icing or anti-icing equipment on the plane, and we would have been illegal to make the flight. I advised Mr. Richard Cullen that we were having to cancel the flight, but I would try to get him a seat on Eastern's DC-3 flight that was properly equipped, and soon ready to leave for New York. Mr. Cullen got very angry about it and reluctantly went on Eastern. I figured this to be the end of my job.

The next morning I went back to Mobile. I went out to the division office, called on Major John Friend and told him what had happened, and my expectation that it was all over for us. Major looked straight at me and said, "Carl, I want to tell you a true story. The company has a fleet of tugboats at Georgetown, South Carolina, and Mr. Cullen on occasion uses one to go deep-sea fishing. On one such trip, he went out in pretty poor weather, and, before long, the captain remarked to Mr. Cullen that they should be turning back because the weather was getting worse. Mr. Cullen said, 'Hell, no, I came out here to fish!' The captain waited a while longer and repeated his view, with Mr. Cullen answering the same way. A third try by the captain and still the same answer, until finally Mr. Cullen said, 'Let's go in now.' When they returned to the dock, he fired the captain!"

New IP kraft mill in
Panama City, Florida,
started; first to make
linerboard on the
Fourdrinier machine.

IP acquired Tonawanda,
New York, mill.

Hammermill Paper
Company introduced the
8-hour day.

1931   1933   ⫸➔

A group of Southern Kraft executives waits to board IP's Lockheed Lodestar corporate plane in 1958. Behind them and immediately in front of the plane stand co-pilot Paul Fearn (l.) and chief pilot Carl Lund (in hat).

Credit: Courtesy Carl Lund,
Reminiscences, 1992.

Major Friend leaned forward and said, "You see, he was testing the captain, and he failed to

uphold his command. Mr. Cullen was testing you, and you held your ground!"

He was right. Mr. Cullen and I became good friends. And I was fortunate to accumulate

32 years of service with the company.

Carl Lund (Corporate Pilot), reminiscences, 1992.

Incorporation of General
Crude Oil Company, later
acquired by IP.

Federal Paper Board
Company, later merged
with IP, returns to prof-
itability.

IP's Moss Point mill started
producing bleached kraft
wrapping papers.

Arizona Chemical devel-
oped new technique to
clean crude liquor
turpentine.

1933   **1934**   **1935**   ⟫+

I started working at International Paper in 1942 at the Single

Service plant in Kalamazoo, Michigan. We were using gluing

machines to make milk containers. Each year as we got raises,

men got a larger raise and we (the ladies) got more speed on the

machines. When I retired in 1965, we were hand-feeding one

million cartons a day.

In the 1950's life was good. The war was over and we were

happy about that, and I enjoyed my job and the friendships

I made. Among my friends were Katie Woodruff, Lorina Ham

and Helen Barringer, a silent screen star fron the 1920s who

worked with me for seven or eight years.

Dollie Keckler, reminiscences.

*Women workers, Kalamazoo,
Michigan, plant, circa 1955. Dollie
Keckler is on the right end of the
back row.*

Credit: Courtesy Dollie Keckler,
Vicksburg, Mississippi.

Passage of Public Utility Holdings Act forced IP to divest itself of most of its hydroelectric power operations.

Floods forced suspension of IP's operations at Livermore Falls, Maine, and York Haven, Pennsylvania.

Richard Cullen named president of IP.

IP's Moss Point, Mississippi, mill developed continuous bleaching to replace batch processes; continuous bleaching was later introduced throughout the industry.

IP's Southern Kraft Corporation started construction of Georgetown, South Carolina, kraft mill.

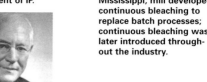

1935   1936

The development of a new release liner for the feminine hygiene market is an example of how IP divisions worked together to make a product that enables customers to save costs, improves our competitive position and is better for the environment. The new release paper was a joint effort by Thilmany, the Androscoggin mill, the Corporate Research Center, and Akrosil Menasha, Wisconsin, and Europe. Akrosil commercialized the product by the end of 1995. Many customers qualified the product in 1996 and 1997, most recently at Procter & Gamble in Japan, qualifying paper from Akrosil Europe.

In this case we developed a product as an IP team using both our paper knowledge and silicone release coating know-how to come up with a lot of added value. The new release paper offers cost savings in material and transport, has a 22.5 percent basis weight reduction with no significant reduction of strength, and produces less waste for both our processes and our customers.

Gert Jan Heemsbergen, Akrosil Europe.

1937

Akrosil advertisement, 1991.

Credit: Courtesy Larry Harris, Menasha, Wisconsin.

Arizona Chemical started
salt cake business in Texas.

Canadian International
Paper sold its large
newsprint mill in Corner
Brook, Newfoundland.

IP's Springhill, Louisiana,
mill substantially completed;
produced bleached kraft
paper pulp in a seven-stage
continuous bleach process.

Masonite Company of
Canada, Ltd. formed by
Canadian International
Paper and Masonite
Corporation; jointly owned
plant built at Gatineau,
Quebec, to manufacture
Masonite hardboard prod-
ucts for sale in Canada and
export markets other than
the United States.

1937   **1938**   **1939**

*Technicians check a recording unit,
part of the computer process
control system installed at the
Georgetown mill, 1963.*

Credit: *International Paper Company
Annual Report for 1963.*

IP's Springhill, Louisiana, mill started production of bleached kraft paper and board.

Beginning of World War II in Europe triggered dislocations in IP's export trade.

IP acquired Agar Manufacturing Corporation, a leading corrugated box manufacturer.

IP's Georgetown, South Carolina, mill installed No. 3 paper machine, making it the world's largest paper mill.

WWII

1940   1941   ≫→

I joined the company in 1963 at the Georgetown mill. I had a degree in electrical engineering and an MBA. I worked on a computer process control project, which was a joint venture between IBM and IP. It was the first computer control project in the company. We used an IBM 1710 computer with an IBM 1620 central processing unit. There was a group of about five of us on the team.

We started on the No. 2 paper machine at Georgetown, which was making IBM punch card stock, because it made the same product day and night, and they wanted to establish measuring techniques. We moved from the paper machine into the pulp mill and the bleach plant. It was really a little bit like flying an airplane the first time, here this monster is running, and all of a sudden you're controlling it. But it was a lot of fun, and we knew we were on kind of the coming thing.

Page Williamson, interview, Memphis Operations Center, Memphis, Tennessee.

Reorganization of IP's corporate structure; Southern Kraft Corporation renamed Southern Kraft Division; International Paper and Power Company terminated.

IP built corrugated container plant in Georgetown, South Carolina.

United States enters World War II.

The U. S. Government implemented price controls for newsprint.

1941   **1942** ➤➤

You're trying to make paper with, say, a 4 percent moisture content. So the paper tester would reach in with a knife and take a sample out without breaking the sheet off, and then he'd run into the lab. You've got to get in there pretty fast because the moisture content is being changed. He would stick it into a moisture sensor and get a moisture reading. And then he'd take maybe six or eight samples—swatches—from the end of the reel, as the reel was turned up and the next reel was starting to go, and he'd run those through the machine. Then he'd come out and tell the papermaker, "You have moisture here, you've got 4.7 percent here and 5.2 there." And the papermaker would try to adjust things to help that out.

They took samples to make other tests, too—they tested for thickness, tearing strength and all those other things.

Victor Oaks, interview, Chicago, Illinois.

CALCULATOR

The Burroughs Calculator was the adding machine of choice in research laboratories until the 1960s, when it was replaced by the electronic computer and the hand-held pocket calculator.

Credit: Courtesy Jay Robertson, Camden, Arkansas.

Strength-testing Kraft paper, Georgetown mill, circa 1946.

Credit: Courtesy Corporate Archives, Purchase, New York.

International Paper began advertising its products in the late 1920s, utilizing the pages of *The International Paper Monthly,* its corporate magazine.

These efforts remained small-scale and were confined to trade advertising until 1960, when IP undertook its first nationwide corporate advertising campaign aimed at a broader audience. Centered around what president Richard C. Doane termed "the power and lasting importance of the printed word," IP's "Send me a man who reads" advertising campaign brought the company highly favorable public recognition. Another corporate advertising campaign, "The Power of the Printed Word," which began in 1979, was aimed at encouraging the public—especially young people—to appreciate the value of written communication. The award-winning campaign, which presented articles written by noted communicators such as novelist Kurt Vonnegut, TV news anchor

Walter Cronkite and actor Tony Randall, was seen by millions of Americans. In another important departure, the company used the occasion of the Apollo 11 flight to the moon in 1969 to launch its first television advertising campaign, sponsoring the Columbia Broadcasting System's round-the-clock coverage of the epic event. More recently, IP's sponsorship of the 1996 Olympic Games in Atlanta, Georgia, and its renowned television and print advertising campaign featuring the children of IP employees, have brought the company national visibility, underscoring the impact of its theme:

"International Paper: We Answer to the World."

"Send me a man who <u>reads</u>!"

Here is what International Paper learned by examining the reading habits of 200 men who spend many of their working hours on planes and trains.

In one week, 100 sales trainees devoted an average of over 4 hours to newspapers, and 3 hours to magazines. These young men travel two to three days out of every week.

And in one week, 100 sales managers—who spend the same amount of time traveling as the trainees do—devoted an average of over 6 hours to reading newspapers, and slightly under 3 hours to magazines. The implication is as clear as print:

Great salesmen keep on reading.

You can be sure both groups are on the best of terms with the traveler's newest companion. The paperback book. Paperbacks are slim and extremely light—easy to squeeze into a suitcase.

Millions of people are reading them. And *not* to the disadvantage of hard-cover books. Hard-cover sales are also on the rise.

Read wherever you can. You'll add a great deal of *pleasure* to the business of living. And whatever your job, *you'll do it better if you read.*

Look what fun and facts you find in paperbacks these days

Paperbacks offer wonderful fun and information to almost everyone.

Children can read about Buffalo Bill, Treasure Island and Mary's little lamb.

Women can choose from 29 books on gardening, 37 on child care, and 90 on cooking. Hi-fi buffs can learn more about woofers and tweeters from 20 different paperbacks on high fidelity.

And armchair detectives can find out whodunit in 29 mystery novels by one author alone!

Paperbacks are sold almost everywhere. They're a great bargain.

Free: Write Box 35, Education Department, International Paper, 220 East 42nd St., New York 17, N. Y., for free reprints of this advertisement.

© International Paper Company 1962

INTERNATIONAL PAPER

Manufacturers of papers for magazines, books, newspapers · papers for home and office use · converting papers · papers and paperboards · ...eing · labels · folding cartons · milk containers · shipping containers · multiwall bags · grocery and spe... ...cks · pulps for industry · lumber, plywood and other building materials

---

How to write with style.

by Kurt Vonnegut

International Paper asked Kurt Vonnegut, author of such novels as "Slaughterhouse-Five," "Jailbird" and "Cat's Cradle," to tell you how to put your style and personality into everything you write.

Newspaper reporters and technical writers are trained to reveal almost nothing about themselves in their writings. This makes them freaks in the world of writers, since almost all of the other ink-stained wretches in that world reveal a lot about themselves to readers. We call these revelations, accidental and intentional, elements of style.

They tell us as readers what sort of person it is with whom we are spending time. Does the writer sound ignorant or informed, crooked or honest, humorless or playful—? And on and on.

Why should you examine your writing style with the idea of improving it? Do so as a mark of respect for your readers, whatever you're writing. If you scribble your thoughts any which way, your readers will surely feel that you care nothing about them. They will mark you down as an egomaniac or a chowderhead—or worse, they will stop reading you.

The most damning revelation you can make about yourself is that you do not know what is interesting and what is not. Don't you yourself...

like or dislike writers mainly for what they choose to show you or make you think about? Did you ever admire an empty-headed writer for his or her mastery of the language? No.

So your own winning style must begin with ideas in your head.

Find a subject you care about.

Find a subject you care about and which you feel others should care about. It is this genuine caring, and not your games with the language, which will be the most compelling and seductive element in your style.

I am not urging you to write a novel—although I would not be sorry if you wrote one, provided you genuinely cared about something. A petition to the mayor about a pothole in front of your house or a love letter to the girl next door will do.

Keep it simple.

As for your use of language: Remember that two great masters...

William Shakespeare and James Joyce, wrote sentences which seemed almost childlike when their subjects were most profound. "To be or not to be?" asks Shakespeare's Hamlet. The longest word is three letters long. Joyce, when he was frisky, could put together a sentence as intricate and as glittering as a necklace for Cleopatra, but my favorite sentence in his short story "Eveline" is this one: "She was tired." At that point in the story, no other words could break the heart of a reader as those three words do. Simplicity of language is not only reputable, but perhaps even sacred. Your rule might be this: If a sentence, does not illuminate your subject in some new and useful way, scratch it out.

Sound like yourself.

The writing style which is most natural for you is bound to echo the speech you heard when a child. English was the novelist Joseph Conrad's third language, and much that seems piquant in his use of English was no doubt colored by his first language, which was Polish. And lucky indeed is the writer who has grown up in Ireland, for the English spoken there is so amusing and musical. I myself grew up in Indianapolis, where common speech sounds like a band saw cutting...

How to read a newspaper.

by Walter Cronkite

International Paper asked Walter Cronkite, for years television's foremost news anchor and spokesman of the need for a free people to keep fully informed, to tell you how your newspaper can help you cope better with your world.

If you're like most Americans, you use TV to keep up with the news. That's how 2/3 of us get 100% of our news.

The problem is that unless something really special happens, we in TV news have to put severe time limitations on every story, even the most complicated and important ones.

Get more than headlines.

So what we bring you is primarily a front page headline service. To get all you need to know, you have to flesh out those headlines with a complete account of events from a well-edited and responsibly... newspaper...

...have a responsi... it. Ours is to... ...accurately...

...keep...

Which is the main story?

You'll always find the main or lead story in the farthest upper right hand column. Why? Tradition. Newspapers used to appear on newsstands folded and displayed with their top right hand quarter showing. They made up the front with the lead story there to...

...lice readers...

You'll always find the second most important story at the top far left, unless it's related to the lead...

...pictures and read the captions. I do the same thing page by page, front to back. Only then do I go back for the whole feast.

The way the front page is "made up" tells you plenty. For one thing, the headline type size will tell you how the paper's editor ranks the story in relative importance. A major crop failure in Russia should get larger type than an overturned truckload of wheat on the interstate, for example.

story. Do you have to read all the stories in the paper? Gosh, no. But you should *check* them all. Maybe the one that appears at first to be the least appealing will be the one that will most affect your life.

News is information, period.

A good newspaper provides four basic ingredients to help you wrap your mind around the news: information, background, analysis and interpretation.

Rule #1 of American journalism is: "News columns are reserved only for news."

What is news? It is information only. You can tell a good newspaper story. It just reports the news. It doesn't try to slant it. And it gives you both sides of the story.

Look out for a lot of adjectives and adverbs. They don't belong in an objective news story. They tend to color and slant it so you may come to a wrong conclusion.

Do look for bylines, datelines and the news service sources of articles. These will also help you judge a story's importance and its facts.

Also weigh its truthfulness by asking: "Who said so?" Look out for "facts" that come from unnamed sources, such as "a highly placed government official." This could tip you off that the story is not quite...

It doesn't look like he needs a bath.

War Production Board froze paper mill production at current levels.

IP began producing military packaging and other products to support the war effort.

Consolidation of Federal Paper Board Company, later merged with IP, under new ownership; John R. Kennedy elected president.

John Hinman elected IP president; Richard Cullen elected chairman of the board.

1942

1943

My personal philosophy in managing was always one in which I wanted to make my presence known out in the facility where people worked and did their jobs. I wanted them to know who I was, and I wanted to know who they were. I wanted them to know that I was interested and concerned about them and their well-being and what went on in the process that they were involved in. Everyone really appreciated me coming through, seeing what they were doing, talking and listening to their suggestions and concerns.

A lot of times in big organizations there's too much "we-them," when it ought to be just "we." The mill is a team, and that team has to be not only the management people, but also the people who are out working on the job— the production workers. You have to be willing to listen, to let them know that their ideas and suggestions are important.

I found that this approach to managing people was a learning process, but one that paid off considerably.

Alan Day, interview, Memphis, Tennessee.

IP's Fort Edward, New York, mill sold to Scott Paper Company.

Agar Manufacturing Corporation's name changed to IP Container Corporation.

End of World War II; most price controls for paper lifted.

IP's Southern Kraft Division developed the first mechanical tree planter.

1944 **1945**

Alan Day was manager at several IP facilities, including the Androscoggin mill in Jay, Maine, which he managed from 1977 to 1982. He later became an IP vice president.

Credit: Courtesy Dennis Gingles, Augusta, Maine.

1945 **1946**

*Annual outing, Storrs & Bement
Company employees, 1946. Carter
Rice acquired Storrs & Bement
in 1953.*

Credit: Courtesy William Boyce,
Erlanger, Kentucky.

Arizona Chemical commercialized tall oil processing.

IP built corrugated container plant in Springhill, Louisiana.

IP acquired Single Service Containers, Inc.

Canadian International Paper's research laboratory incorporated as Industrial Cellulose Research, Ltd.

IP celebrated its 50th anniversary.

1898   1948

1948

ANNUAL OUTING OF STORRS-BEMENT CO EMPL AT "STOW" COUNTRY CLUB. MAY. 25, 1940.

I was employed for many years in the accounting department of Carter Rice Paper Company. Some of the happiest memories I have were the Christmas parties and summer outings where we would meet the people from other branches of the company—other people we would talk to on the telephone but didn't know what they looked like!

Bernice J. Dever, reminiscences.

Strathmore Paper
Company introduced
Strathmore fine paper
grades.

IP built corrugated
container plant in
Wooster, Ohio.

IP's conservation foresters
arranged forestry exhibit
programs and timber
cutting demonstrations
which were attended by
thousands of people in IP
locales across the South.

IP's Quarter Century
Society reorganized.

1948 **1949** **1950**

Back before 1976, when we had the Southern Kraft Division and the Northern

Division, all of our mills in the South were under one contract. So we would go

to Jackson, Mississippi, once every three years and there would be delegates there

from 10 mills plus all of the international union officials and management

people from all of the mills. There would probably be 300 people in the room.

The Union asks for a dollar, hoping for a quarter. We offer a dime hoping to

settle for 15 cents. All the rest is window dressing.

Jim Gilliland, interview, Mobile, Alabama.

*Union label, International
Brotherhood of Paper Makers.*

Credit: Courtesy Al Bowerman,
Jay, Maine.

New IP mill started in Natchez, Mississippi, the first dissolving pulp mill to produce 100 percent hardwood pulp by innovative processes developed by IP.

IP's Camden, Arkansas, mill introduced the first continuous digester in North America as part of a pilot project based on Kamyr machinery incorporating technology developed at IP's Mobile, Alabama, research laboratory.

IP built liquid packaging plants in East Point, Georgia and Kansas City, Kansas.

IP's Natchez, Mississippi, mill was in commercial production and being doubled in size.

Union management contract negotiations Southern Kraft Division mills, circa 1967.

OVERLEAF

Mike Shanks and Andrew Blevins inspect SuperTree™ pine seedlings at IP's nursery near Selma, Alabama, 1993. SuperTree seedlings are planted on IP's forestlands or are sold or donated to other landowners.

Carter family in New
Zealand reorganized its
wood products business,
formation of Carter
Consolidated, Ltd., later
merged into Carter Holt
Harvey, of which IP later
acquired a majority of
shares.

IP's Mobile, Alabama,
research group laboratory
moved into new quarters.

IP built liquid packaging
plant in Kalamazoo,
Michigan.

Formation of Reliable
Paper in Milwaukee,
Wisconsin, later part of
IP's distribution business.

1951   **1952**

*Hammermill Paper Company
Band, Erie, Pennsylvania,
circa 1925.*

Credit: Courtesy Elizabeth Wasielewski,
Erie, Pennsylvania.

IP started liquid packaging plant in Youngstown, Ohio.

Federal Paper Board Company, later merged with IP, went public with a $3.4 million stock offering.

Formation of International Paper Company Foundation.

IP's board of directors created the office of chairman of the board, the chief executive office of the company. John Hinman was elected chairman and Richard Doane president.

IP built liquid packaging plants in Minneapolis, Minnesota, and Philadelphia, Pennsylvania.

1953   1954   ⏩

How those papermakers can toot! We could sit in our spruce-covered booth and listen to them whoop it up all afternoon as there was no business done at the fair while they were playing, for their music was too good to miss.

William K. Myers, "Following the Fairs with Our Mulch Paper," *The International Paper Monthly*, February 1929, p. 20.

IP built corrugated
container plant in Geneva,
New York.

IP commited to a
multimillion dollar R & D
program to develop the
plastic-coated Pure-Pak
container.

IP's Mobile, Alabama,
research laboratory developed Supercell AO-2
bleached hardwood kraft
market pulp.

Commercialization of IP's
low-wax milk carton
stock.

IP started corrugated
container plant in
Zellwood, Florida.

1954   1955

I came out here to the Natchez mill that first day, and nobody
would even come close to me. I was like a pariah. I came on in,
and I said, "I'm gonna do it or bust."

I was in the machine shop and they put me with one man in
particular the first couple of days. He was a big man—I mean, a
big, strong man. We were putting a big piece of equipment in
the lathe, the biggest lathe we've got. You have to really tighten
it down to keep it from falling out. And he said, "Okay, gal, I
want you to tighten this up. Take this wrench and tighten this
up. And I don't want it to fall out either."

I said, "Okay, I tightened it up." I mean, I got down on it.

When he rolled it around he couldn't budge it one way or the
other. He couldn't tighten it any more.

When I did that, it seemed like things changed.

Nancy Eidt, interview, Natchez, Mississippi.

Federal Paper Board
Company, later merged
with IP, listed on the New
York Stock Exchange.

IP included among com-
panies comprising the
Dow Jones Industrial
Average.

IP acquired Long-Bell
Lumber Company.

IP's Southern Kraft
Division entered the
newsprint field when its
105,000 ton newsprint
machine began operation
at Mobile, Alabama.

IP started liquid packag-
ing plant in Turlock,
California.

INTERNATIONAL PAPER COMPANY
LONG-BELL
D I V I S I O N

1956

*Jessie Ruckus and Nancy Eidt,
Natchez mill, 1975.*

Credit: Courtesy Lillie E. DeShields,
Natchez mill.

IP wants to stay in business in the years ahead. As long as we can manage our timberlands in a biologically sound way, we will be looked upon favorably by the American people. Whenever we turn around, big as we are, we meet the public, and it is always a public that uses the land and is watching how we treat it.

Jim Buckner, *Viewpoints*, Summer 1980, p. 17.

IP's Camden, Arkansas, mill started the first commercial continuous digester in North America.

IP's Southlands Experiment Forest in Bainbridge, Georgia, was established to conduct research on a wide range of forestry issues, including forest genetics and to develop the SuperTree™.

IP started corrugated container plants in Edinburg, Texas and Houston, Texas.

IP built liquid packaging plant in Raleigh, North Carolina.

1956   1957

After I got to be the corporate director of research, and became a vice-president, I decided to start promoting the fact that the International Paper Company needed a real, solid, honest-to-goodness research department and facility. And finally it bore fruit when I made a presentation to the board of directors one day to establish the Corporate Research Center at Sterling Forest, New York. The reception was very positive. The main question concerned how we would be able to staff it. I explained that the Sterling Forest area had several research facilities already established there, and so I felt that it would be a good environment for our technical people. I got several million dollars to do it with and we finally spent about $15 million over the next couple of years to build it. It's still a fine place, I think.

John Gilbert, interview, Mobile, Alabama.

A 60,000-ton per year
machine for machine-
coated publication papers
began operations at IP's
Hudson River mill in,
Corinth, New York.

IP converted 15 percent of
its own output.

Completion of IP's Pine
Bluff, Arkansas, mill.

IP started corrugated
container plants in
Auburndale, Florida; Fond
du Lac, Wisconsin; and
Mason, Ohio.

1958

*John Gilbert (l), vice president and
corporate director of research, and
William G. Dodge, general manager,
Corporate Research Center, 1966.*

*Architect's rendition of proposed
Corporate Research Center, 1966.*

Credit: *International Paper
Annual Report for 1966.*

A 50,000-ton per year machine to produce light-weight papers was installed at IP's Pine Bluff, Arkansas, mill.

Beckett Paper Company acquired by Hammermill Paper Company, which was later acquired by IP.

IP sales top $1 billion for the first time.

IP started liquid packaging plants in Miami, Florida, and Caracas, Venezuela.

Off machine coater was introduced at the Moss Point, Mississippi mill to produce label paper.

1959

To me, one of the most gratifying events during my career was the development of a genetic improvement in the quality of trees. We started the industry—IP was the leader.

There are a number of things that came out of it. The most spectacular, I guess, is the reduction in the number of trees that get a disease. Resistance to disease is an inheritable factor, and it has resulted in a major improvement in the net growth of trees that are genetically superior. But there are other things that came out of it. The rate of growth is a significant one. The density of growth is a significant one. And the quality of growth—all of these things are part of the result of the genetic improvement. So, that's been a great source of satisfaction to me.

Fred C. Gragg, interview, Mobile, Alabama.

Fred C. Gragg (l), vice president and general manager-woodlands, Southern Kraft Division, and Lawrence J. Kugleman, vice president and general manager-Woodlands, inspect a test plantation of slash pine trees grown from genetically improved seed at the Southlands Experiment Forest in Bainbridge, Georgia, 1966.

Credit: *International Paper Company Annual Report for 1966.*

IP produced polyethylene-coated milk carton stock at the Pine Bluff, Arkansas, mill.

IP's common stock was split 3:1.

International Paper organized the Overseas Division to coordinate and promote the export of IP products.

Arizona Chemical completed refining plant in Springhill, Louisiana.

IP started corrugated container plants in Phoenix, Arizona, and Omaha Nebraska.

IP started liquid packaging plants in Framingham, Massachusetts, and Versailles, Kentucky.

1960

Because of the nature of the business we're in—some of our pulps are pretty specialized—we are becoming more quality conscious. We run what we call "quality partnerships" with our customers. Whenever we have a problem with production or they might have a problem with our product, we talk about it. We have

IP and W.R. Grace Company started bagasse paper mill at Cali, Colombia.

IP built bleach plant at Georgetown, South Carolina, mill, enabling the mill to produce white papers.

Richard Doane elected chairman of IP's board of directors; Lamar Fearing elected IP president.

IP received patent for Turfiber, a wood-cellulose mulch used in the establishment of grass over large areas.

1961

very frank exchanges on where we are and where we need to go. We share our problems and arrive at solutions. It's a total team approach—a very open relationship that really produces dividends.

Developing these customer quality partnerships has been one of the most important changes that's taken place here over the last eight or nine years. It makes things work so much better.

David Hatton, interview, International Paper UK Ltd., Leatherhead, Surrey, England.

Cali, Colombia mill, partly owned by IP, started operations.

Oswego New York, mill acquired by Hammermill Paper Company, later acquired by IP.

Hammermill Paper Company acquired Western Newspaper Union, a paper products wholesale organization.

IP started corrugated container plant in Chicago, Illinois.

IP's Georgetown, South Carolina, mill installed one of the first paper mill computer systems.

1961

1962

When we first arrived at Kwidzyn, every day at 2 p.m. shift change, there was a bicycle traffic jam as nearly 500 workers left to go home. Today there is still a traffic jam at shift change — but now it is with cars.

The economy of Kwidzyn (40,000 people) has grown by leaps and bounds. From 150 local shops, stores and businesses to over 900 today. The town is a microcosm of (Poland's economic growth and) activity.

Poland is going to do okay and International Paper-Poland is proud to have been a part of it. The entrepreneurial spirit is alive and well. From supporting the economy to supporting the community — hospitals, schools, etc.

Dave Bailey, International Paper, Poland, 1996.

IP started Sales Training Program.

The Lord Baltimore Press opened a plant at Springdale, Ohio.

IP's Creative Marketing Center established.

Federal Paper Board Company, later merged with IP, completed a recycled paperboard mill in Versailles, Connecticut.

IP built corrugated container plants in Presque Isle, Maine; Pittsburgh, Pennsylvania; Springdale, Ohio; and Statesville, North Carolina.

IP started liquid packaging plant in Longview, Washington.

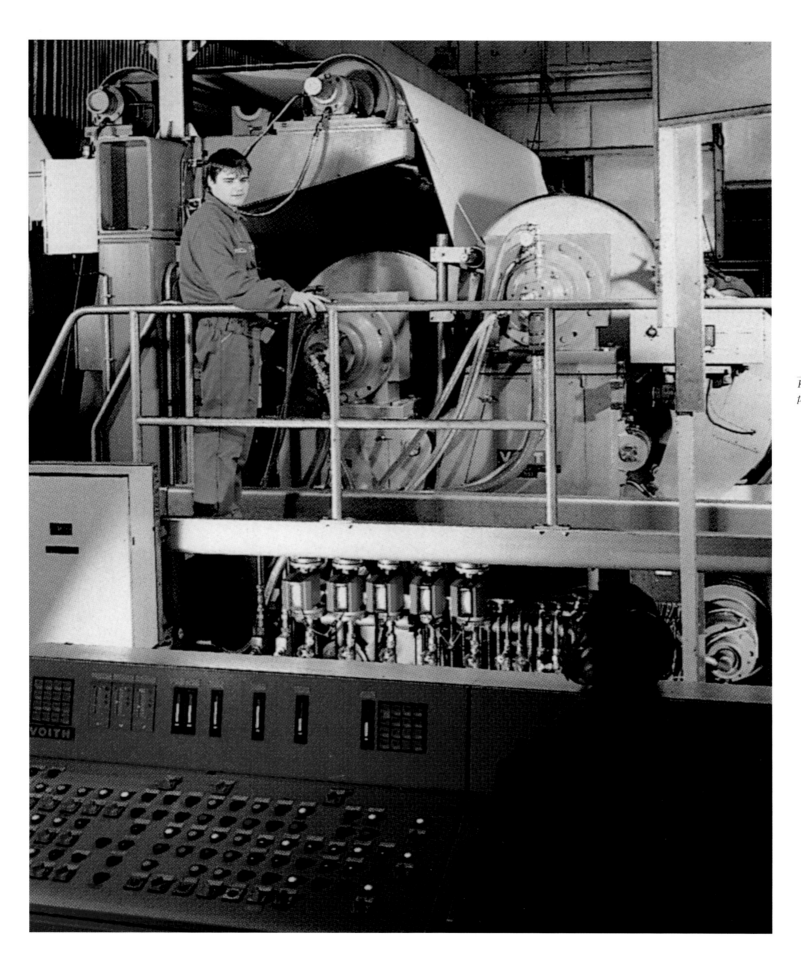

Kwidzyn is Poland's largest bleached pulp and white papers manufacturer.

Credit: Courtesy International Paper, Poland.

IP's Erling Riis Research Laboratory at Mobile, Alabama, introduced pulping technology that led to a substantial increase in the use of oak as pulpwood in the Southern mills.

IP built corrugated container plant in Dallas, Texas.

IP introduced process to control root rot, a major killer of pine trees.

My father worked at IP. He was a general mechanic in the maintenance department and also a president of one of the local unions. IP afforded him an employment opportunity which, in turn, allowed my parents to provide us with an education. That's not true just for my brother and me. The company afforded a lot of people in this area opportunities they would have never had.

Margaret Steele, interview, Natchez, Mississippi.

Wayne Steele.

Credit: Courtesy Lillie E. DeShields, Natchez mill.

Margaret Steele, human resources specialist, Natchez, Mississippi, mill, 1997.

In some of the mills during World War II, ladies came in and took the place of men and *ran* those jobs. And those ladies were still there when the war was over, and they stayed there, and from that time on, it's been ladies helping run those operations—and that was a pretty manual thing back then. It was doing quite manual work—*quite* manual work.

Roger Matlock, interview, Shreveport, Louisiana.

Pulp machines at IP's
Natchez, Mississippi, mill
were working full time on
pulps for the production
of Tyrex viscose tire yarn.

Sales of Federal Paper
Board Company, later
merged with IP, exceeded
$100 million for the first
time.

IP's Container Division
introduced the Ice-Pak®
poultry box.

IP converted 20 percent of
its own output.

IP's foil-laminated Pure-
Pak carton was in
commercial production.

1964   1965

André Dollé.

Credit: Courtesy Christophe Morange,
Aussedat Rey.

J'ai vu deux fois dans ma vie arriver les Américains. La première fois c'était en novembre 1942. J'avais 6 ans et j'habitais en Afrique du Nord, á Arzew. Mon père était basé au Fort du Nord, un fort aménagé en batterie côtière. Durant la nuit, nous avons été réveillés par des coups de feu: ce n'était pas les Allemands, mais le débarquement des troupes anglo-américaines. Mon père parlant couramment l'anglais, bon nombre d'invités se sont succédé á la maison.

La seconde fois, en 1989, leur arrivée a été annoncée lors du rachat d'Aussedat Rey par International Paper. Je n'en ai vu que très peu. Par contre, il est une chose que j'ai pu constater, puisque j'étais concerné par certains investissements, c'est que l'on est á présent obligé d'être plus rigoureux et sélectifs dans les projets. Cela oblige les dirigeants à tous les niveaux à etre plus conscients des problèmes de terrain, à mieux connaître les process, à être plus pragmatiques. Nous avons pu constater enfin à Maresquel une relance dans la recherche de produits nouveaux. Cela est positif, à mon avis.

Maintenant, je pense surtout à l'avenir, plus le mien, mais celui de l'usine de Maresquel. Si l'esprit pionnier qui caractérise les Americains pouvait s'allier à celui que nous avons à Maresquel, alors l'avenir s'annonce sous d'heureux auspices!

André Dollé, reminiscences.

IP's Androscoggin mill in Jay, Maine, was operational.

Lock Haven, Pennsylvania, mill acquired by Hammermill Paper Company, later acquired by IP.

Hammermill Paper Company built pulp mill in Selma, Alabama.

IP started corrugated container plants in Bay Minette, Alabama, and Guadeloupe, French West Indies.

IP started liquid packaging plant in Los Angeles, California.

Interior of Maresquel mill.

Credit: Courtesy Christophe Morange, Aussedat Rey.

I have seen the Americans arrive twice in my lifetime. The first time was in November 1942. I was six and was at that time living in Arzew in North Africa. My father was stationed at Fort du Nord, a coastal fortification. One night while we were in bed, we were awakened by gunfire. It wasn't the Germans as we thought, but the landing of Anglo-American troops. As my father spoke fluent English, a good number of Americans were invited to our house.

The second time was in 1989, after the acquisition of Aussedat Rey by International Paper was announced. Being involved as I was in several investments, I soon noticed how the IP way coming over here from the United States led us to be more rigorous and selective in our ventures. Managers at every level now have to be more aware of problems on the shop floor; have a better understanding of the processes; and be more pragmatic. The result has been that we have seen a revitalization in new product development at our Maresquel mill. In my opinion this has been very positive.

Now, above all, I look to the future—not mine, but that of the Maresquel mill. If the pioneering spirit which characterizes the Americans can unite with that of the employees of Maresquel, the future promises great things.

André Dollé, reminiscences.

Edward B. Hinman
elected IP president and
chairman.

IP started corrugated
container plants in
Baltimore, Maryland;
Detroit, Michigan; and Las
Palmas, Canary Islands.

IP started Vicksburg,
Mississippi, mill.

IP closed its Niagara Falls,
New York, mill.

Acetate dissolving pulp
commercialized at IP's
Natchez, Mississippi, mill.

IP bought Federal Paper Board for the good things Federal did, not just to come in and say they could do a better job. Federal prided itself on trying to do as well in every aspect of the business as you can. I think that's IP's philosophy, too.

It (the merger) was a good thing for both sides. They meshed well because there was not a lot of overlap. Federal was big in a segment of the business—bleached board—that IP was not very big in. Putting the pieces of the puzzle together, it probably couldn't have been any better of a match.

Louis Grissom, interview, Riegelwood, North Carolina.

A Federal Paper Board employee monitors production on high-speed converting equipment.

Credit: *Federal Paper Board Annual Report for 1995.*

IP acquired Davol Inc., a major supplier of health care products.

First commercial use of the vertical twin-wire former at Canadian International Paper's Three Rivers, Quebec, mill.

IP began its first all-plastic operation at a consumer packaging plant in Litchfield, Illinois.

Frederick Kappel named chairman of IP.

IP began construction on new Ticonderoga, New York, mill on Lake Champlain to replace the Lower Falls facility.

IP started corrugated container plant in Murfreesboro, Tennessee.

1968 ▶▶

I've always been interested in the natural environment. And when I actually thought about what I wanted to do, I realized I wanted to help people be aware of the impact their activities have on it.

One of the first things I did in my job as an environmental engineer at Carter Holt Harvey was to coordinate and organize a project in which the National Institute of Water and Atmospheric Research researched the effects of our operations on stream ecosystems. They studied the actual and potential environmental effects of harvesting and roading operations—that is, our "moving dirt" operations—on forest stream life. They looked at the way we do things, and at our internal guidelines. The result of the study showed the state of the stream ecosystem to be more like a native forest system than one which would be found in an agricultural setting.

Karen Shaw, Carter Holt Harvey Ltd, Tokoroa, New Zealand.

IP opened Corporate Research Center in Sterling Forest, New York; closed Glens Falls, New York, research laboratory.

Start of IP's Dynamic Forestry program, large-scale replanting program throughout the South.

IP's Acadia Forest, the world's first LASH (Lighter Aboard Ship) vessel, completed its maiden voyage to Europe.

Bodcaw Company started kraft mill in Pineville, Louisiana, later acquired by IP.

IP built wood products plants in Nacogdoches, Texas, and Wiggins, Mississippi.

1969

In 1985-1986, having dismantled a good deal of the corporate staff organization which built up in the 1970s, we found ourselves in that rather large corporate headquarters on 45th Street in New York City. I can recall someone saying that we had built that facility to house about 2,200 people, and we found ourselves rattling around in the place with about 950 people. And it just didn't make sense to stay there longer. At that point the company started to search for an alternative. And so looking for a place that would make more sense started the search that ultimately led us here to Memphis for our operating headquarters. It turned out to be a perfect location and a pretty good move for the company.

Memphis Operations Center, 1987.

Credit: Courtesy Highwoods Properties, Inc., Memphis, Tennessee.

Thilmany Paper Company acquired by Hammermill Paper Company, which was later acquired by IP.

IP started corrugated container and liquid packaging plant in Tallman, New York.

IP started corrugated container plant in Modesto, California.

IP announced a four-year $100 million air and water protection program.

IP's first nonwoven fabrics plant opened at Lewisburg, Pennsylvania.

1970

Culturally, for those of us from New York who moved to Memphis, it was a change—no question about it. Probably not so much for those of us that worked here as it was for our families that were uprooted and brought down here. But when we worked in New York, you lived anywhere from 30 to 50 miles away from midtown Manhattan—in different parts of the metropolitan area—and you never really had a chance to socialize with your fellow workers or their families on an after-hours basis. Down here it changed—because physically you could do that, but also because there was a need. I mean, we were all thrown into a strange city. And while the city did everything it could to make us feel welcome, still a lot of the New York families banded together in those early days. There were parties and get-togethers, support groups among the spouses, and things like that. It really helped a great deal to have that sort of support grow up among people who weren't used to doing things like that because they came from the New York area where you just didn't do that.

The other thing that I found rewarding here in Memphis is that unlike New York, where your chance to really be part of the community in which you lived was pretty limited, many of us have become involved and do things in the community. It's given us a chance to do something we wouldn't have been able to do had we still been in New York.

Charles Connelly, interview, Memphis Operations Center, Memphis, Tennessee.

Aussedat Paper Company, a leading French paper producer, merged with Rey Chemicals and Cellulose Company to form Aussedat Rey, later an IP subsidiary.

IP closed York Haven, Pennsylvania, mill.

Paul Gorman elected chairman, president, and chief executive officer of IP.

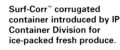

Surf-Corr™ corrugated container introduced by IP Container Division for ice-packed fresh produce.

1970 **1971**

The Sheridan School had about two acres that we leased to them so that they could put their sign up and take classes out there and do whatever they wanted to do on that land. It was only about a mile away from the school. This was one of several school forests that IP helped sponsor. They would take kids out there and measure trees or maybe learn to identify them. We'd also let the kids do some cutting under close supervision so they'd get some feel for it.

IP also had a "Pilot Forest Program" where we'd have landowners, all kinds of community groups, schools, come over for a tour and a demonstration of what could be done to improve their land by planting trees or thinning trees or stopping fires.

This is one of the biggest things that we did over the years—educating everyone we possibly could.

Harold S. Winger, interview, Mobile, Alabama.

IP closed several obsolete facilities, including the old Ticonderoga, New York, mill, known as Lower Falls mill.

Start of IP's Texarkana, Texas, mill.

IP sales reached the $2 billion mark.

IP sold its interest in the Donald Bren Company, a developer of planned communities.

Federal Paper Board Company, later merged with IP, bought paper mill in Riegelwood, North Carolina.

Dedication ceremony for the Sheridan School Forest near Sheridan, Arkansas, 1958. Harold S. Winger, who was then district forester for the Sheridan District, is in the center of the photograph, wearing a plaid shirt.

Credit: Courtesy Harold S. Winger, Mobile, Alabama.

Machine room, Otis mill, 1909.

Credit: Courtesy Don LeClerc,
Wausau Papers, Livermore Falls, Maine.

1898

INTRODUCTION

On the threshold of the 21st century, International Paper is a diversified, global company with manufacturing operations in the Western Hemisphere, Europe, Asia and South Africa. Its international presence is the result of long-term changes that evolved since the company's founding in 1898. Starting as a pulp and paper company based in the Northeastern part of the United States, IP expanded into Canada and the American South during the 1920s. Three decades later the company began expanding beyond North America. This was followed during the 1980s by the acquisition of subsidiaries operating in Europe, South Africa and Asia.

ORIGINS AND GROWTH, 1898-1940

Incorporated in Albany, New York, on January 31, 1898, International Paper was a merger comprised of 17 pulp and paper mills.* Production facilities ranged from a small mill in Turners Falls, Massachusetts—which produced 11 tons of paper per day—to the Hudson River mill in Corinth, New York, one of the most advanced in the industry with a daily output of 150 tons. Holdings

also included 1.7 million acres of timberland in the Northeastern states and Canada. During its early years, IP was the nation's largest producer of newsprint, supplying 60 percent of all newsprint sold in the United States and exporting to Argentina, England and Australia.

The company became an industry pioneer under the leadership of Hugh Chisholm, who served as president from 1898 to 1907. Milestones included the construction of the first laboratory in the American pulp and paper industry in Glens Falls, New York, the industry's first collective bargaining agreement and an innovative timber harvesting system that protected young trees. Operating in the Northeastern United States, the heartland of the turn-of-the-century pulp and paper industry, IP employed some of the nation's most experienced papermakers, many of whom had honed their skills during decades of shop floor labor. These workers knew their pulpwood grinders and paper machines inside and out and rarely needed the advice of managers, who usually concentrated on administrative and financial matters.

The company's newsprint business declined after 1913, when the United States Congress eliminated tariffs on low-cost Canadian imports, which flooded U. S. markets, eroding IP's market share. Moreover, the company became embroiled in a labor conflict in 1921 that disrupted its system of collective bargaining. IP was subsequently led by Archibald Graustein, president from 1924 to 1936. Graustein reinvigorated the company's newsprint operations by forming Canadian International

*Prior to the present International Paper history project, there has been considerable confusion about the exact number of paper mills that merged on January 31, 1898, to form IP. Various authors have counted up to 22 original mills. In-depth research has determined that the actual number of original International Paper mills was 17; see Paper Trade Journal, Feb. 5, 1898. Other authors may have been confused by the fact that several other paper mills *intended* to join IP but did not merge on January 31; see Paper trade Journal Jan. 1, 1898: "It was expected that Piercefield Falls Pulp and Paper Company, of Piercefield Falls, N.Y., 30 tons; the Gould Paper Company, Remington Paper Company, 30 tons, of Watertown, N.Y., with Wilder & Co., of Olcott Falls, N.Y., 40 tons, would also be in shape to go in under incorporation papers, but it was found that they could not arrange matters in a reasonable time, so that these mills will, in all probability, be taken in later, after the organization has been perfected."

Paper, an IP subsidiary that acquired vast tracts of timberland in Canada and constructed some of the world's largest newsprint mills in the Province of Quebec. Within the United States, the company diversified into Southern kraft paper production by acquiring two mills in Bastrop, Louisiana, and one in Moss Point, Mississippi, and by building new mills in Camden, Arkansas, and Mobile, Alabama. Consolidating its operations in the Northeastern part of the United States, IP sold or closed several older mills and converted the remaining ones from newsprint to book and bond grades. The company also built up an extensive hydroelectric power business in the Northeast and Canada. This venture had to be dissolved when Congressional legislation prohibited the combination of manufacturing operations and electrical power production.

In addition to providing jobs in many small mill communities, the company created an extensive system of employee benefits. This included employee stock options, company housing in several locations and the Employees Mutual Benefit Association, which offered life insurance and disability programs to employees. IP also hired nurses who rendered first-aid services in the mills and served as community health care providers. In 1937, the company resumed negotiations with labor organizations representing pulp and paper workers, machinists, electricians and other workers employed in company mills.

The Great Depression of the 1930s marked a difficult period. Like most manufacturing companies, International Paper suffered severe financial losses due to the unprecedented economic downturn, forcing the com-

pany to reduce output and lay off workers. In addition to selling off poorly performing subsidiaries, the organization weathered these hard times by introducing a range of new products and, later, by branching out into the packaging business. In 1931, IP became one of the first paper companies to manufacture linerboard on the Fourdrinier machine, which produced inexpensive, high-quality grades for use in corrugated containers. Major customers for this product included a leader in the corrugated container industry, the Agar Manufacturing Corporation, which was acquired by IP in 1940. This transaction made the company one of the first integrated linerboard manufacturers in the American pulp and paper industry.

Other efforts to develop new business followed the same pattern. In 1939, IP pioneered bleached kraft grades for folding cartons, tags and file folders and supplied the first bleached kraft paper grades that were suitable for milk carton production. The company sold the bulk of its milk carton board output to Single Service Containers. Determined to expand its presence in the converting sector, IP acquired Single Service in 1946 and later turned it into an integrated liquid packaging operation. The company also laid the foundation for its specialty products business during the Great Depression. During the early 1930s, it formed Arizona Chemical as a joint venture with the American Cyanamid Company. Arizona Chemical refined crude liquor turpentine, a by-product of the sulfate pulping process, and later became a specialty chemicals producer with operations in the United States and overseas. In 1939, Canadian International Paper teamed up with the Masonite Corporation to build a hardboard products plant in Gatineau, Quebec. Almost five decades later, IP acquired Masonite with operations in the United States, Europe and South Africa. The quest for new technologies, products and markets during the Great Depression of the 1930s was initiated by Richard Cullen, who served as president from 1936 to 1943, and as chairman of the corporation from 1943 to 1948.

VIEW FROM THE TOP, 1940-1960

The early 1940s marked a watershed in the history of the company. In 1941, International Paper completed a large-scale reorganization that recapitalized the company and simplified its corporate structure. During World War II, International Paper converted some of its manufacturing operations to the production of military items. These included the V-1 Box, an ultra-strength container developed by IP that replaced wooden crates for the shipment of military supplies. Featuring five layers of moisture-proof kraft board laminated with insoluble adhesive, the V-1 Box underwent rigorous testing, in which it was left to soak in the ocean surf for 24 hours and then dropped repeatedly on a concrete floor. Using large amounts of recycled paper, IP also manufactured kraft cases for the transportation of gun shells and hundreds of other military items. Nitro-cellulose for explosives was made from dissolving pulps produced by Canadian International Paper's mills.

The postwar era witnessed unprecedented growth and prosperity. John Hinman, who led the company as president from 1943 to 1954 and as chairman from 1954 to 1961, reduced its debt to zero and increased dividend payments. During his tenure, International Paper estab-

lished a research laboratory at Mobile, Alabama, and the Southlands Experiment Forest at Bainbridge, Georgia, which developed IP's SuperTree™ through selective breeding of genetically superior pine trees. In 1950, the company started a dissolving pulp mill in Natchez, Mississippi, that was the first to use 100 percent hardwood, and started a paper mill in Pine Bluff, Arkansas, producing newsprint, milk carton grades and lightweight white papers. Other milestones of the postwar era included a multimillion dollar research program launched in 1955 to develop the plastic-coated milk carton, and the formation of the International Paper Company Foundation, a grant-making organization that supports education in IP communities. Converting operations increased with the construction of new liquid packaging and corrugated container plants, and with the acquisition of the Lord Baltimore Press, a leading folding carton company.

In 1956, IP acquired the Long-Bell Lumber Corporation in an attempt to diversify into markets outside paper production and conversion. Although the Federal Trade Commission initially argued that this transaction violated anti-trust legislation, the merger was eventually approved. The struggle with federal authorities over the Long-Bell acquisition, however, convinced IP to proceed cautiously with further efforts to expand beyond pulp and paper. As a result, IP became less diversified than major competitors during the 1950s and early

1960s, leaving it more exposed to the highly cyclical market for newsprint and kraft paper products. The company tried to address the diversification problem during subsequent years, but a viable solution was not implemented until the 1980s.

The late 1950s marked the beginning of International Paper's expansion overseas. The company had been a major exporter for decades and maintained sales offices in London, Paris, Zurich and Johannesburg. In 1959, it added the first overseas manufacturing operations through joint ventures with container companies in Israel, Germany, Greece and Italy. The same year it organized a new subsidiary and built a liquid packaging plant in Caracas, Venezuela. It also acquired major shares in a bagasse paper mill in Cali, Colombia; converting operations in Arecibo, Puerto Rico; and a folding carton plant in Mexico City. Also in 1959, International Paper first achieved $1 billion in sales.

Under the leadership of Richard Doane—elected president in 1954 and chairman in 1961—International Paper further developed its pulp and paper business. Responding to growing competition that resulted in a decrease of domestic market share, Doane established a creative marketing center and launched an innovative sales training program. On the manufacturing side, IP added new mills in Vicksburg, Mississippi; Gardiner, Oregon; and Jay, Maine. In 1962, the Georgetown, South Carolina, mill became one of the first in the pulp and paper industry to install computerized information and process control systems. Improving its converting operations, IP built and acquired liquid packaging, corrugated container and folding carton plants in the United States.

International expansion continued throughout the 1960s. Overseas manufacturing operations acquired during the 1960s included corrugated container plants in Catania, Italy; Bilbao, Spain; and Arles and Mortagne, France. These facilities improved International Paper's presence in the European market. The company also built new corrugated container plants in Pomezia, Italy; Guadeloupe, French West Indies; and Las Palmas, Canary Islands.

International Paper entered a critical period in the late 1960s. Controlling valuable and debt-free assets that had been built up over decades, IP witnessed an era of an unprecedented number of mergers and acquisitions. To avert a hostile takeover and tackle IP's diversification problem, Edward Hinman—elected president and CEO in 1966—increased the company's indebtedness and acquired specialty businesses, including a major real estate developer and a manufacturer of medical products. However, like many leading corporations of the late 1960s that diversified into markets that were unrelated to their core businesses, IP found it difficult to integrate its recent acquisitions and most were sold a few years later. A recession in the pulp and paper market meanwhile led to a 30 percent drop in the company's earnings in 1970, producing additional financial hardships.

Despite these difficulties, International Paper scored a number of important successes during this era. Its nonwoven fabrics division, which built a plant in Lewisburg, Pennsylvania, made IP an important nonwoven fabrics producer and laid the groundwork for Veratec, a specialty business launched in 1987. Another major initiative of the late 1960s and early 1970s was the construction of the Corporate Research Center at Sterling Forest, New York. This facility has pioneered important manufacturing and environmental technologies as well as innovative products during subsequent decades. IP also built state-of-the-art pulp and paper mills in Ticonderoga, New York, and Texarkana, Texas.

Edward Hinman was succeeded by Frederick Kappel who served as chairman of International Paper's board of directors from 1969 to 1971. Formerly chairman of American Telephone & Telegraph, Kappel was the first leader of International Paper since Phillip Dodge (1912-1924) who had spent most of his career with another company.

Streamlining its operations during the 1970s, International Paper phased out several facilities and improved its marketing organization. These tasks fell to Paul Gorman—who served as chairman from 1971 to 1974—and his successor J. Stanford Smith, who led the company until 1980. During their respective tenures, IP closed or sold older mills in Livermore Falls, Maine; Panama City, Florida; and Springhill, Louisiana. A large-scale corporate reorganization in 1976 replaced the Southern Kraft Division and the Northern Division with functional business units: white papers, consumer packaging, industrial packaging, wood products and specialty packaging. In each business unit, production managers were encouraged to think as marketing and financial managers, and vice versa. As a result, strategic changes in a unit's manufacturing operations were made with a keen eye on earnings and sales.

MEETING THE CHALLENGES OF CHANGE, 1980-PRESENT

This restructuring led to a major new initiative in the 1980s, when IP launched a large-scale overhaul of its mills. Led by Dr. Edwin Gee—who served as chairman from 1980 to 1985—IP conducted in-depth studies of mills and plants. The Bastrop, Louisiana, mill had to be closed in 1982. Other mills received extensive upgrades in a $6 billion capital improvement program that included a complete reconfiguration of the Georgetown, South Carolina, mill. The program phased out inefficient linerboard operations and switched to more profitable bleached paper products. The program also included the reconfiguration of the Mobile, Alabama, mill from newsprint and kraft grades to white papers. These mill reconfigurations enhanced production efficiency and contributed to a 5 percent cost decrease in per-ton production of white papers from 1982 to 1988. Financial resources for the corporate capital program were raised through the sale of Canadian International Paper, General Crude Oil Company and other subsidiaries, stock offerings and loans. In addition to reconfiguring existing facilities through the corporate capital program, International Paper built a highly efficient containerboard mill in Mansfield, Louisiana, which helped the company reduce containerboard production costs by 18 percent in a six-year period.

Mill construction and conversion during the 1980s went hand in hand with quality improvement and product development initiatives. Recognizing that product quality and customer service were key to success in the highly competitive pulp and paper market, IP launched a quality management program that sensitized employees to customer needs, gave them more opportunities to improve product quality, and helped shift decision-making authority to the lowest appropriate level. Moreover, the company introduced a variety of new products that enjoyed considerable popularity with customers. In 1989, IP introduced Classic Pak®, a container for the poultry industry that captured a 20 percent share of this market.

The decade from the mid-1980s to the mid-1990s marked a period of unprecedented expansion when sales more than quadrupled, reaching $20 billion in 1996. This trend reflected the growth of high-value product lines, enhanced by the acquisition of the Hammermill Paper Company in 1986. This $1.1 billion transaction was engineered by John Georges, chairman from 1985 to 1996. In addition to a rich tradition in fine paper production and nine mills, Hammermill brought invaluable marketing experience into the partnership. Recognized as the "best-known name in paper,"

Hammermill had developed a distribution network and a reputation for quality that were unrivaled in the American pulp and paper industry. As a result of the merger, IP learned valuable marketing lessons and Hammermill improved the profitability of its manufacturing operations. Hammermill's extensive distribution network later became the foundation for ResourceNet International, a large-scale marketing organization that sold a wide variety of products made by IP and other leading companies. Operating in 250 locations at the time, the distribution operation sold graphic arts supplies and equipment, printing paper, industrial packaging, janitorial and maintenance supplies, retail packaging and related products. ResourceNet International was renamed xpedx in 1998.

One year after the Hammermill acquisition, a labor conflict emerged at International Paper. In an effort to control production costs, the company had negotiated a number of agreements with the United Paperworkers International Union and others to eliminate premium pay for work performed on Sunday and holidays. However, strikes took place at three mills and there was a lockout at a fourth. The strikes and lockout ended in the fall of 1988. In 1993, the company and the union signed a "peace accord" and agreed to return a positive relationship.

In the late 1980s, International Paper devised a viable solution to its diversification problem. In the pulp and paper industry, whose core business was highly cyclical, a secure foothold in less-volatile markets was necessary to maintain a healthy balance sheet when earnings from paper products declined. IP had learned painful lessons during the late 1960s, when it made acquisitions that did not fit into the overall organization. Determined to avoid this mistake, IP strengthened its position in markets for specialty products that were related to its core business but less cyclical in earnings than the pulp and paper market.

In 1988, for example, the company acquired the Masonite Corporation, modernized its manufacturing facility in Laurel, Mississippi, and later built an additional plant in Ireland. These investments fulfilled their purpose. In 1996, when the printing papers business stagnated, earnings in IP's specialty panels business grew at double-digit rates. IP derived similar benefits from other specialty businesses, including chemicals and petroleum, nonwoven fabrics and silicone-coated products.

The late 1980s and early 1990s marked a period of international expansion. Prior to this era, the company had exported a significant share of its products to overseas markets but most of its manufacturing operations were located in the United States, the world's largest paper market. During the 1980s, however, overseas demand for paper rose sharply with the introduction of office copiers, computer printers and fax machines. In Europe, paper consumption per person rose at an annual rate of 3 percent, compared to 1 percent in the United

States. In 1989, International Paper acquired two European paper companies: Zanders Feinpapiere AG, Germany's leading producer of coated papers that had been founded in 1829; and Aussedat Rey, a diversified French manufacturer of office copying paper, specialty panels and related products whose origins date back to the 18th century. In 1992, IP expanded its European presence with the acquisition of Kwidzyn, Poland's most modern paper mill, which subsequently was expanded and upgraded.

During the early 1990s, IP also gained a major presence in the Pacific Rim, where it established over time a majority shareholder status in Carter Holt Harvey of New Zealand. Founded in the 19th century, Carter Holt Harvey became a leading manufacturer of pulp, paper, tissue, containerboard and wood products operating primarily in New Zealand and Australia. It also acquired a presence in a Chilean energy and forestry company, COPEC. Carter Holt Harvey's diversified holdings centered around a core business in wood products fit well with IP's overall organization and corporate philosophy. IP acquired majority shareholder status in Carter Holt Harvey in 1995.

The most recent chapter in the history of International Paper, which began with John Dillon's election as chairman and CEO in 1996, was still unfolding when the company approached its centennial. One of the leaders of IP's corporate strategy development during the 1980s and early 1990s, Dillon's philosophy emphasizes customer focus, low-cost production, technological innovation, workforce diversity, and employee involvement in running the business.

At the beginning of Dillon's tenure as chairman, IP extended its long tradition of community involvement by providing building materials for the reconstruction of churches that had been destroyed by a series of arson attacks. Moreover, IP was a major sponsor of the 1996 Summer Olympic Games in Atlanta Georgia.

One of Dillon's first business objectives was the successful integration of Federal Paper Board into the International Paper family. Federal merged with IP in March 1996 in a $3.5 billion transaction that included mills in: Augusta, Georgia; Riegelwood, North Carolina; Versailles, Connecticut; the Tait mill in Inverurie, Scotland, as well as extensive packaging and wood products operations. The merger has exceeded its financial expectations.

Also in 1996, International Paper opened the new Cincinnati Technology Center, a major facility that includes, among many operations, pilot project plants for development work in printing, packaging and extrusion coating. The Cincinnati Technology Center continues some of the functions of the Erling Riis Research Laboratory which was phased out.

Under Dillon's direction, the company undertook a thorough evaluation of its businesses leading to decisions that would guide the allocation of capital and set new requirements for acceptable levels of profitability. As a result of this analysis, the company announced, in mid-1997, a performance improvement plan that would include the sale of $1 billion in assets.

THE IP WAY

As in the past, International Paper is committed to continuous improvement in everything it does and the key is the people who make up the company. In 1898, a typical paper mill was run by skilled workers who knew more about pulp production, paper machines and product quality than anyone else in the organization. One hundred years later, International Paper is committed to becoming a High Performance Organization, a company with a greater degree of teamwork and greater decision-making power delegated throughout the organization in order to better satisfy customers and beat the competition.

Employees sharing their ideas and experiences to improve the business is part of what has come to be called "the IP Way." More formally, "the IP Way" includes a commitment to be a global leader and earn an excellent return. It includes being the company of choice not only for customers but employees, shareholders and suppliers.

In 1998, as International Paper enters the new millennium, its success in fulfilling its vision will depend on the ability to continue its legacy as a company of employees who think and act with creativity, energy and, most of all, the drive to succeed.

1998

David G. Cabe monitors the No. 16 paper machine from the control room at the Riverdale mill in Selma, Alabama. The machine is the largest, fastest and widest paper machine of its kind in the world.

International Brotherhood of Pulp, Sulfite and Paper Mill Workers merged with United Papermakers and Paperworkers to form United Paperworkers International Union.

Lord Baltimore Press and Muirson Label integrated into what later became IP's Folding Carton and Label Division.

IP built corrugated container plant in Putnam, Connecticut.

Observance of IP's 75th anniversary.

Production interrupted by a 12-week strike at five Canadian International Paper mills and a four-week strike at IP's converting operations.

1972 **1973**

During World War II, IP used its widely scattered resources to become a primary supplier of wet-strength linerboard. In 1942, the industrial strength of the United States was concentrated on supplying arms and munitions to the armed forces. Packages that could endure under wet conditions or that could be floated into beachheads on the surf were a necessary part of that "supplying." Therefore IP was authorized to build the Georgetown No. 3 machine to supply wet-strength linerboard for the packages.

The company gave the Camden mill the project of developing and optimizing the manufacturing process for wet-strength linerboard. The absolutely best wet-strength liner was made using American Cynamid's Parez 607 resin in solution added to the stock at the fan pump. The joker was that the 607 had to be put into solution in muriatic (hydrochloric) acid, but there were no tanks, pipes, or pumps available that could handle the acid. Therefore, a wooden tank made with tongue-and-groove lumber was built up in the machine-room trusses (so that it would clear the machine-room cranes), and 13-gallon carboys of acid were hoisted up and dumped in the tank. The resin was mixed in the acid with boat paddles. (I was a boat paddle operator.) Quality wet-strength paper was made in this manner, so that Georgetown could build its resin make-up and handling system while its No. 3 machine was being built.

Are we a great company, or what!

Charlie Power, reminiscences.

IP established Folding
Carton and Label Division.

Oven-Pak microwave oven
tray introduced by IP.

IP closed liquid packaging
plants in Youngstown,
Ohio, and Longview,
Washington.

J. Stanford Smith elected
chairman of the board and
chief executive officer of IP.

1974

*Wet-strength linerboard produced at
the Georgetown and Camden mills
was used to produce these "V
boxes" for American servicemen
and women overseas.*

Credit: *International Paper Company
Annual Report for 1943.*

IP acquired wood products plant in Madison, New Hampshire.

Landowner Assistance Program started by IP to assist private landowners with technical expertise in scientific forest management.

Startup of first molded door facing line at Masonite Towanda, PA mill, later an IP subsidiary.

IP's Ticonderoga, New York, mill commercialized oxygen bleaching technology developed at Corporate Research Center, Sterling Forest, New York.

IP built corrugated container plant in Bellusco, Italy.

1974

The Olympic Games give every nation the opportunity to bring its own values, cultures and traditions to an international platform. By bringing world-class athletes (and their governments) together, the Olympics serve as a bridge by which both concerns and, more importantly, solutions can be shared. This is a time when all countries can put aside their differences, even in times of unrest, and enjoy a period of harmony. The Olympic Games are much more than athletes, medals or even world records. They are a link, a keystone, a glue that holds the international world together, encouraging a more peaceful society.

Michael Caldwell, Memphis, Tennessee.

The Olympic Games promote peace in the world by bringing together a variety of countries and cultures. These countries are brought together in the spirit of competition.

Many men and women come together to try and win, to make new friends. The sports involve no cultural boundaries. The barriers of language and daily differences are forgotten as the participants focus on their sport.

When we look at our common goals, we are able to come together in peace.

Chasity Charnell Woods, Russellville, Arkansas.

1975

"A peace wave is coming."

Her name is Chelsea Cupp, she's nine years old and she believes that the Atlanta Games are about more than just sports. Can the Summer Games help foster global peace? That's the question we posed (in the form of an essay contest) to the children of International Paper's more than 50,000 U.S. employees. Chelsea's essay was a winner.

A peace wave is coming.

When we play by the rules and treat others with respect, our sportsmanship cultivates harmony.

As a team we can accomplish anything, and if we work together …peace will reign.

To read all of Chelsea's essay — and others — visit our Web site at http://www.ipaper.com. And enjoy the Atlanta Games before the peace wave surges on toward Nagano, Japan.

Chelsea Cupp, age 9, from Atlanta, Texas, who won the Gold prize in the seven to 10 age group, is the granddaughter of William E. Moore, Jr., an employee at the Texarkana mill. All contest entrants were related to IP employees.

Credit: Courtesy International Paper Company and KCSA Public Relations, New York, NY.

© 1996 International Paper

Atlanta 1996
OFFICIAL SPONSOR
1996 OLYMPIC GAMES

INTERNATIONAL ⒜ **PAPER**

We answer to the world.

Start of a two-year, $175 million expansion of IP's Androscoggin mill in Jay, Maine.

IP acquired General Crude Oil Company.

Wood products plant in Maplesville, Alabama, built by Hammermill Paper Company, later acquired by IP.

IP built corrugated container plant in Russellville, Arkansas.

John R. Kennedy Jr. elected chief executive officer of Federal Paper Board Company, later merged with IP.

1975

I started to work for International Paper in the late 20s. John Hinman decided that I should continue my timberland activities after I graduated from Dartmouth College. IP did not have a formal training program, so I was left to develop my own. I decided I should learn more about logging costs and forest management. A sawmill owner in the Province of New Brunswick was logging on IP timberlands in the vicinity of Frederick. He agreed to turn me over to other sawmill owners in this area.

At that time "lumberjacks" were sleeping on pine-spruce boughs with a roll-bottom wool blanket. An individual was provided with a single top blanket. We slept in wool long-sleeve underwear. Meals were provided in the kitchen of the logging camp—breakfast 6 a.m.; first lunch mid-morning; 2nd lunch mid-afternoon; and full supper after the day's work. Food provided was prunes, baked beans, corned beef. We added fresh trout or salmon where available, molasses, applesauce, and tea and/or coffee.

Lawrence J. Kugelman, reminiscences.

Reorganization of IP's corporate structure. Southern Kraft Division and Northern Division replaced by business units:

- Consumer Packaging
- Industrial Packaging
- Specialty Packaging

- White Papers
- Wood Products and Resources

IP's Corporate Research Center developed a line of wet-formed products for formed fabrics operations.

IP introduced Fresh-Shield packaging system, a polyethylene-coated folding carton designed to prevent moisture loss while retaining freshness and flavor.

IP started multiwall bag plant in Wilmington, Ohio.

Wood products plants in Eatonton, Georgia, and Georgetown, South Carolina, started by IP.

1976

Lean-to used for sleeping quarters, logging camp, Restigouche Woods, New Brunswick, circa 1930. A man inside the lean-to is making a bedroll out of pine boughs.

Credit: Courtesy Corporate Archives, Purchase, New York.

Canadian International
Paper's Gatineau mill in
Quebec commercialized
sulfonated chemimechani-
cal pulp as a low-cost
substitute for kraft pulp in
newsprint furnish.

$175 million expansion of
IP's Androscoggin mill in
Jay, Maine, completed.

$215 million plant
improvement program
started at Riegelwood,
North Carolina, mill by
Federal Paper Board
Company, later merged
with IP.

Dr. Edwin A. Gee elected
president of IP.

1976   **1977**   **1978**

*Mr. And Mrs. James H.
("Whistler") Williamson and their
six children, circa 1985. Thomas
("Tweeter") Williamson is in the
back row, second from the left.
"Tweeter" recalled that he got his
nickname from the men who had
worked with his father at the Pine
Bluff mill, since they decided that
he was too small to be another
"Whistler."*

Credit: Courtesy Thomas Williamson,
Queen City, Texas.

A $155 million expansion program of IP's Texarkana, Texas, mill completed.

IP sold its Otis mill in Livermore Falls, Maine, to the James River Company.

IP built multiwall bag plant in Pittsburgh, Kansas.

IP sold a $763 million interest in General Crude Oil Company.

IP sold Panama City, Florida, mill to Southwest Forest Industries.

1979

I guess you could say that International Paper has fed and clothed me for all of my life, because my father worked for the paper mill. He worked for International Paper all his life, at the Pine Bluff mill. I think he put in about 48 years with the company. He stayed with it for 48 years because he saw International Paper as a growing company, as really a *family*-oriented company.

IP furnished my wife, also—I met her at the mill. She was working in the labor gang and I was in the electrical shop, and she would come through the shop periodically and sweep the shop, and she was in there one day and I offered her some doughnuts. And it just went from there and six months later we were married, and we're still married to this day.

So they furnished me with, I guess, everything I have, except my sons. I did a little bit on my own, after working on company time.

Thomas ("Tweeter") Williamson, interview, Texarkana mill, Texarkana, Texas.

Thomas and Nancy Williamson and their sons Jake (top) and Matt (bottom).

Credit: Courtesy Thomas Williamson, Queen City, Texas.

I helped work on the project celebrating International Paper Company's 50th Anniversary, hooking up ice cream machines and soda pop machines in empty lots all over the town of Bastrop.

I wouldn't mind helping do it for the 100th Anniversary.

Vernon Sawyer, recorded story, IP Centennial Phone Bank.

Newspaper advertisement, The Bastrop Clarion, *June 11, 1948*.

Credit: Courtesy Corporate Research Center, Sterling Forest, New York.

AN INVITATION

TO ALL THE PEOPLE OF

Bastrop AND Vicinity

To attend an open house

Wednesday, June 16th & Thursday, June 17th

DURING THE WEEK OF JUNE 14-19 WE WILL CELEBRATE THE 50th ANNIVERSARY OF THE FOUNDING OF INTERNATIONAL PAPER COMPANY.

ON WEDNESDAY, JUNE 16th, AND THURSDAY, JUNE 17th,

WE ARE HOLDING *OPEN HOUSE* FOR ALL OUR FRIENDS AND NEIGHBORS. WE WOULD BE VERY PROUD TO HAVE YOU VISIT THE MILL, WATCH US AT WORK AND SEE THE THINGS WE MAKE.

PROGRAM: 9 a.m. TO 5 p.m.

GUIDES will conduct groups through the plant as they arrive, explaining each step of the process of papermaking and the conversion of paper into some of its products.

SPECIAL EXHIBITS will display products of the Bastrop and Louisiana Mills, the Bagpak Multiwall Sack Plant, the Single Service Milk

Container Plant, of the Company's other mills, and of customers.

FREE PARKING facilities will be available at the West Side School.

SPECIAL BUSES providing free transportation to and from the plant will leave West Side School beginning at 9 A. M.

We hope you will be our guests

BASTROP AND LOUISIANA MILLS

Southern Kraft Division

International Paper Company

Bastrop Milk Container Plant

Single Service Division

International Paper Company

Bastrop Multi-Wall Sack Plant

Bagpak Division

International Paper Company

Bodcaw Company
acquired by IP.

IP's Springhill, Louisiana,
mill closed.

IP started liquid packag-
ing plant in Edmonton,
Alberta, Canada.

IP built sawmill and ply-
wood plant near Gurdon,
Arkansas; acquires wood
products plant in Whelen
Springs, Arkansas.

1979

There was what they called a "sorting gap" where they sorted the wood for International Paper. The wood, as it came down the river, was divided into channels. And, essentially, each stick that came down was looked at and decided whose wood it was. And they could tell because you stamped the wood with what they called a "stamping hammer."

The wood came down the river, and you had men out there on booms, and they were looking at this wood and hitting it with a pike pole and pushing it over into this channel or that channel. That was the way the wood was handled.

Mac McLean, interview.

MARKING HAMMER:
Used to mark logs in Maine, this stamping hammer bears an "IP" brand.

Credit: Courtesy John Sutton,
Stratton, Maine

Dr. Edwin A. Gee elected chairman of IP's board of directors.

Reorganization of IP's Wood Products and Resources Group.

IP built corrugated container plant in Carson, California.

IP started liquid packaging plant in Santiago, Dominican Republic.

Wood products plant in Morton, Mississippi, acquired by IP.

1980

Sorting gap, Rastigouche River, New Brunswick, Canadian International Paper Company, circa 1930.

Credit: Courtesy Corporate Archives, Purchase, New York.

IP sold Canadian International Paper for $900 million.

Start of IP's $60 million plywood and lumber manufacturing plant in Springhill, Louisiana.

Start of IP SuperTree™ nursery in Texas.

IP completed wood products plants in New Boston, Texas, and Springhill, Louisiana.

IP started liquid packaging plant in Perugia, Italy.

Reorganization of IP's Manufacturing Technical Services.

1981

Ich würde unter'm Strich sagen, daß die Verbindung von Zanders und IP eine erfolgreiche Verbindung ist. Das ist nicht nur einseitig. IP ist wichtig für Zanders weil es moderne Managementmethoden hier 'reinbringt, und wir brauchen das. Die Finanzkraft eines so riesigen Konzerns ist auch sehr hilfreich. Aber wir als Zanderianer haben IP auch eine Unmenge zu geben, was IP auch anerkennt. Wir haben einen enorm grossen know-how was Papertechnik und Streichereitechnik angeht. Wir machen hier Produkte die so schnell kein anderer erzeugen kann, weil wir eben so tüchtig sind.

Helmut-Josef Mertens, interview, Bergisch-Gladbach, Germany.

Paper machine No. 5 Reflex mill, Düren, Germany.

Credit: Heinz Koch, *Aus Der Geschichte Eines Unternehmens.*

Zanders Feinpapiere AG's first board of directors, (from left) H. Mathias, Dr. W. Stammen, P. Dauscha, H Halfwassen and H.W. Zanders

Credit: Heinz Koch, *Aus Der Geschichte Eines Unternehmens.*

The bottom line is that the partnership between Zanders and IP is quite successful. It's not a one-way-street, of course. IP is important for Zanders because it brings modern management techniques into our operations, and we need those. The financial resources of such a huge corporation are also very helpful. But we as Zanders people have something to contribute as well, and IP recognizes that. We have enormous technical know-how as far as papermaking technology and coating technology are concerned. We manufacture products here that nobody else can make successfully because we're simply very good at what we're doing.

Helmut-Josef Mertens, interview, Bergisch-Gladbach, Germany.

Shutdown of IP's Bastrop, Louisiana mill.

An IP SuperTree™ nursery established in South Carolina.

McEwen Lumber company acquired by Hammermill Paper Company, later acquired by IP.

Start of construction of Kwidzyn mill in Poland, later acquired by IP.

IP closed liquid packaging plant in Minneapolis, Minnesota.

Wood products plant built in Tuscaloosa, Alabama, by Hammermill Paper Company, later acquired by IP.

1982

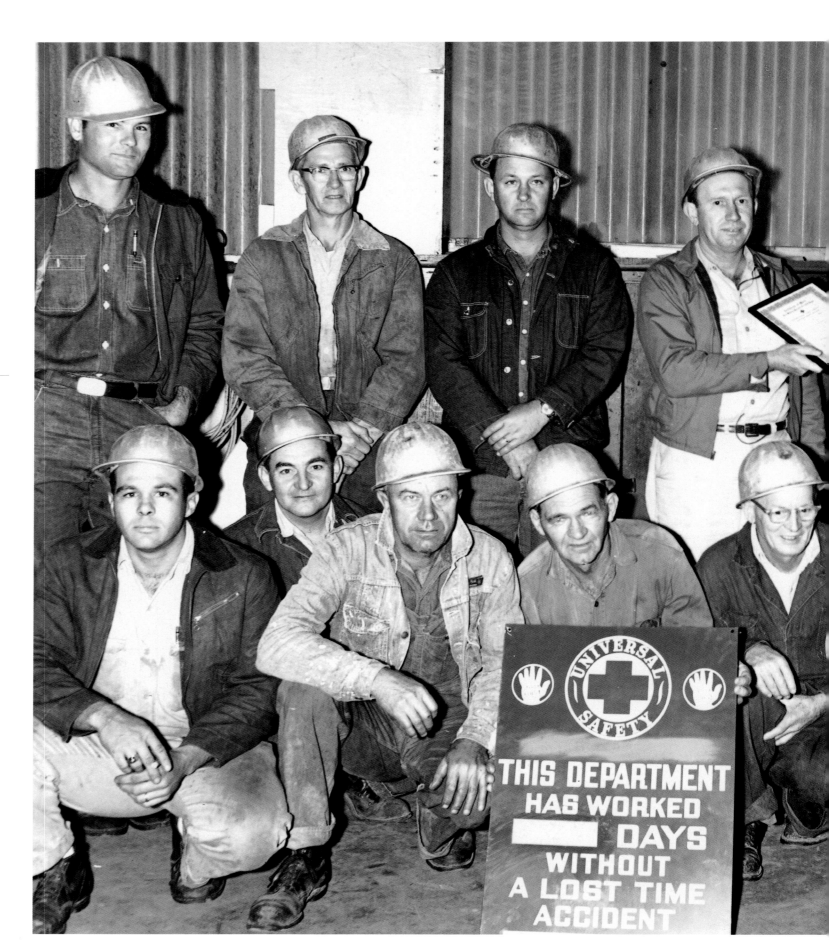

Machine shop crew, Moss Point mill, November 1964.

Credit: Courtesy Robert Burns, Pascagoula, Mississippi.

Conversion of IP's
Georgetown, South
Carolina, linerboard
machine to uncoated
white paper machine,
major element of
a $500 million reconfigu-
ration program at the
mill.

IP's multiple mill group
labor contract was dis-
solved; henceforth each
mill negotiates its own
separate contracts.

IP started Quality
Improvement Process.

Wood products plant in
Pleasant Hill, Missouri,
built by IP.

1983   1984

The greatest achievement that I can remember at the Springhill mill was back in 1975, when we reached two million hours without a lost-time accident. I mean, what they did when that hour came—this happened to be about 11 o'clock one night—they blew the whistle, the steam whistle there, over and over and over, for about 30 minutes. The whole town could hear it. And, you know, it just made everybody feel good to just feel part of it.

And that's way back then. Now we're doing even better. We didn't stop there—now you hear people having lots better safety records than that.

Roger Matlock, interview, Shreveport, Louisiana.

Having worked three million safe hours without a lost-time injury as of February 1997, the 850 employees of IP's Natchez mill surpassed that milestone at 5:00 p.m. on August 22, 1997, when they reached four million safe hours.

Credit: Courtesy Lillie E. DeShields, Natchez mill.

John A. Georges elected chairman of the board of IP.

Creation of IP Timberlands, Ltd., a limited partnership that managed most of IP's timber resources.

IP acquired full ownership of Arizona Chemical.

Augusta, Georgia, mill and other facilities acquired by Federal Paper Board Company, later merged with IP.

Beacon Paper joined IP's distribution organization.

1985

One of the things that I'm really proud of having accomplished as a forester is the development of aerial fire control. In 1945, IP began acquiring fairly large tracts of land in central Mississippi, and all these lands without exception were thoroughly cut-over and burned-over properties. Our main objective was to restock them with growing timber. In order to do that, we had to control fire.

We developed an aerial fire control organization so that it was controlled not necessarily from the fire towers, but from a pilot in a plane. He controlled the

Vic Logan (l.), wood procurement superintendent for the Natchez mill, and John Tyler, Canton Division forester, with central fire control airplane, Madison, Mississippi, circa 1950.

Credit: Courtesy J. R. ("Toby") Tobermann, Plano, Texas.

fire control crews and took care of all their problems that arose during their fires. We had the airplane we operated, we dispatched our fire crews from the plane, and we controlled them from the air. We flew planes quite a few hours every day during every day of fire danger. I think that we were about the first in Mississippi to do anything like that.

John Tyler, Mobile, Alabama.

IP sales surpassed $5 billion for the first time.

Reconfiguration of IP's Mobile, Alabama, mill completed.

IP built corrugated container plants in Shreveport, Louisiana, and Stockton, California.

Federal Paper Board Company, later merged with IP, started $1.1 billion expansion program at its Augusta, Georgia, mill.

1986

LAND LINE SIGN
Signs such as this were posted on IP property boundary lines both to protect company forestlands from wildfires, and to remind the public that everyone in the community is impacted by the economic loss when fire destroys timber.

Credit: Courtesy Frank Taylor, Plano, Texas.

IP moved its corporate headquarters from New York City to Purchase, New York, and its operations center to Memphis, Tennessee.

Arvey Corporation and Black Hawk Paper joined IP's distribution organization.

IP's nonwoven fabrics division was expanded and renamed Veratec.

IP acquired Masonite Corporation.

MASONITE
CORPORATION

1987   **1988**

The Madison lumber mill deals only with Eastern White Pine.

We have over 25 local loggers who bring in our logs. The logs

are debarked and the muddy ends are steamed clean.

Lumber is either air-dried or dried in kilns. If the lumber goes

into the kilns, it will take an average of six days to dry. If it goes

to the air dry yard, it can take anywhere from four months to

one year to dry, depending on the weather.

There are 60 of us to keep the operation going.

Colleen S. Whiting, Madison lumber mill, Madison, New Hampshire.

*Employees of the
Madison lumber mill, 1997.*

Credit: Courtesy Colleen S. Whiting,
West Ossipee, New Hampshire.

IP's sales increased 23 percent to $9.5 billion.

Arizona Chemical, an IP subsidiary, acquired Bergvik Kemi in Sandarne, Sweden.

Saalfeld Paper joined IP's distribution organization.

IP acquired Aussedat Rey, a major French paper and wood products company.

1988   **1989**

Sono piu di venti anni che lavoro nella divisione confezionamento liquidi della International Paper. In questo periodo di tempo, abbiamo vissuto molti cambiamenti technologici

I've been involved in the liquid packaging business for over 20 years. During that time we have been a part of great technological changes. When we first started the liquid packaging business we had almost nothing. We had to develop the product, the aseptic equipment, the material that is used by those systems, and the technical people. So the technological changes have been quite dramatic.

Pierluigi Locchi, IP Italy, interview.

importanti. Quando abbiamo cominciato a lavorare nell'ambito del confezionamento asettico, non esisteva particamente nulla. Abbiamo dovuto sviluppare il prodotto, il macchinario asettico, il materiale da utilizzare con queste macchine ed addestrare il personale tecnico. Quindi, posso affermare che i cambiamenti tecnologici sono stati radicali.

Pierluigi Locchi, IP Italy, interview.

Carter Holt Harvey acquires New Zealand Forest Products, Ltd.

Dixon Paper joined IP's distribution organization.

IP acquired part ownership of Carter Holt Harvey, a New Zealand-based forest products company.

Dillard Paper, Leslie Paper and Wayne Paper joined IP's distribution organization.

Cherry-Burrell, a leading liquid packaging equipment manufacturer, acquired by IP.

IP starts liquid packaging plant in London, Ontario, Canada; starts liquid packaging plant in Kingston, Jamaica.

1990 **1991**

Few of us boys wanted to be soldiers or cowboys or policemen. To be a riverman and go down with the drive was the stated or secret ambition of most of us. To ride a heaving log through white water, to steer a bateau down Fifteen-Mile Falls, to break a jam anywhere—these were the most important things one could hope to do. What we wanted, in that time and place, was a cant dog, a pair of new caulked boots, and a fast-moving stream of logs.

For us, logging camps had all the magic of the Land of Oz. Half-savage places remote from town, yet alive with shouts and the sound of bells and creaking runners, they seemed like stars in the vast forest night and mystery of spruce and fir and hemlock. The forest was dark enough, but never quiet for long. At night it snapped and crackled and boomed from bitter cold. By day it echoed from ax and saw, with only a momentary pause when a falling wedge went home and a big, tall spruce came swishing down to deep silence in the snow.

Stewart H. Holbrook, *Yankee Loggers: A Recollection of Woodsmen, Cooks, and River Drivers* (1961), pp. 10-11.

IP acquired Kwidzyn mill near Gdansk, Poland.

Aussedat Rey, an IP subsidiary in France, completed a plant modernization program that doubled its pulp output capacity.

Zanders Feinpapiere AG in Germany started a new paper machine.

IP started liquid packaging facility in Plant City, Florida.

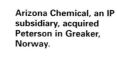

Arizona Chemical, an IP subsidiary, acquired Peterson in Greaker, Norway.

Consolidated Packaging and Western Paper Company joined IP's distribution organization.

1992

Log runners watching for jams, Jessup's River, Speculator, New York, circa 1950.

Credit: Courtesy Dennis Gingles, Augusta, Maine.

Ingram Paper
Company and J.B.
Papers, Inc., joined IP's
distribution organiza-
tion.

IP consolidated its distribution business into
ResourceNet International
(now xpedx) with more
than 250 locations in
North America.

IP spent $94.7 million on
research and development.

IP commercialized
Elemental Chlorine-Free
bleaching.

1993

Je suis tres heureux que l'on m'ai donne la possibilite de travailler a l'usine de St. Priest, en France, construite par International Paper pous le condittionnement des liquides. Je suis employe dans l'atelier extrusion de l'usine.

J'au toujous travaille en equipe. Mes collegues de travail sont dynamiques, hautement qualifies et ont une connaissance poussee de leur machines et du processus de transformation. C'est un travail agreable et tres enrichissant. Il vous faut interagir avec toutes sortes de gens et savoir vous adapter a toutes sortes de personnalites. Masi quand vous travaillez avec une bonne equipe-comme la notre-tout se passe sans probleme.

**Louis Nuziére, interview,
Saint Priest, France.**

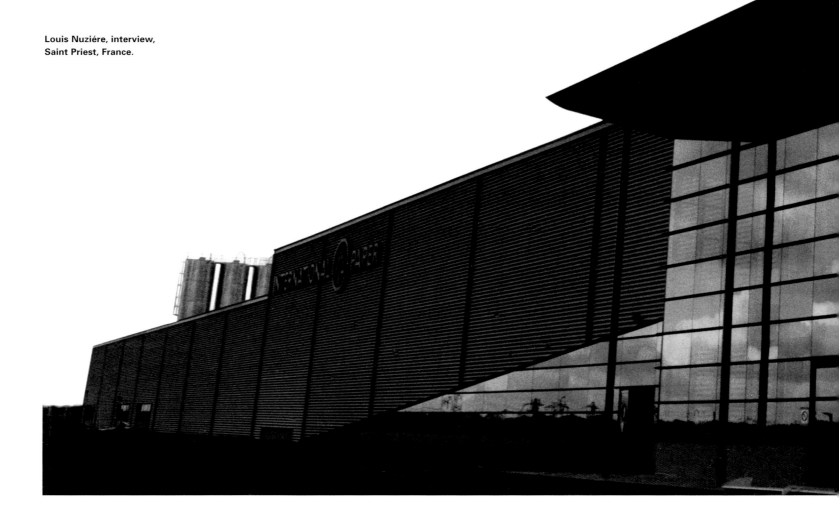

IP established positions of president-IP Latin/South America and president-IP Asia.

Kirk Paper Corporation and Ogi/Kif joined IP's distribution organization.

IP increased its ownership in Carter Holt Harvey, a New Zealand-based forest products company, to 50.1 percent.

Carpenter Paper and Seaman-Patrick Paper Company joined IP's distribution organization.

1994　　　　　　　　　　**1995**　　　　　　　　　　➤

I was very pleased to have been given the opportunity to work at the factory in Saint Priest, France, which International Paper built for liquid packaging. I am employed in the factory's extrusion section.

I've always worked as part of a team. The people I work with are dynamic and very skilled on the machines, and very knowledgeable about the manufacturing process. It is very satisfying and enjoyable. You have to be able to interact with, and adapt well to, a variety of different people and personalities. But when you have a good team—as is ours—everything runs well.

Louis Nuziére, interview, Saint Priest, France.

International Paper Company (Europe) Ltd.'s liquid packaging plant in Saint Priest, a suburb of Lyon, employs some 100 people.

Credit: Courtesy Caroline De Saint Romain and Jean-André Moise, International Paper Company (Europe) Ltd., Saint Priest, France.

Completion of major
expansions at IP mills in
Selma, Alabama, and
Mansfield, Louisiana.

John T. Dillon was elected
IP chairman and CEO.

Federal Paper Board
Company merged with
IP in a $3.5 billion
transaction.

IP built a new Masonite
mill to manufacture
molded door facings at
Carrick-on-Shannon,
Ireland.

IPT announced sale of
general partnership interest of 300,000 acres of
timberland in Oregon
and Washington to R-H
Timberlands.

1995   1996

I started with International Paper in the payroll department at the Georgetown mill in 1937. In 1943 I went through Cadet Air Force training in California and received my wings in April. In May 1943, I received my orders to go overseas. My first stop was Gander Field, Newfoundland. On my way up I thought it would be smart—crazy—to fly over the mill in Georgetown at a very low altitude, because I didn't think they would stop me on my way to combat.

It turned out I flew over the mill and filled the yard with employees because my altitude was—I hate to say—probably less then 300 feet over the mill. It was a crazy stunt for a crazy pilot to do. But I loved IP and I wanted to tell all my friends "goodbye," and I thought that was the proper way to do it.

William A. Johnstone, recorded story, IP Centennial Phone Line.

Global Standard Paper and Taussig's Graphic Supply joined IP's distribution organization.

IP announced a performance improvement plan that included the sale of $1 billion in assets.

ResourceNet International changed its name to xpedx.

IP celebrates its 100th anniversary.

Aerial view of Georgetown mill, Georgetown, South Carolina, circa 1943.

Credit: Courtesy Bob Gifford, Georgetown, South Carolina.

In the century since it had its start in 1898 as a major supplier of newsprint in the United States, International Paper has grown to become the global leader of the paper and forest products industry. It manufactures and distributes thousands of products for customers in more than 130 countries around the world. The company's major manufacturing lines include business, coated and specialty papers; paper and specialty pulps; industrial and consumer packaging; lumber, plywood, oriented strand board and other wood products; siding, door panels and other building materials; tissue products; nonwoven fabrics; and resins, tall oil and other chemical products and derivatives. IP's merchant distribution businesses supply industry, wholesale and end users on three continents—North America, Europe, and Asia—with a vast array of products from world-class manufacturers.

"It certainly is a pleasure for those of us who worked through the difficult 30s to now see IP not only the largest, but also one of the most successful, in the forest products industry. I'm also grateful to others who gave me additional opportunities far beyond my original hopes and aspirations. I can only wish the company the best of success in the years ahead." Roscoe C. Masterman

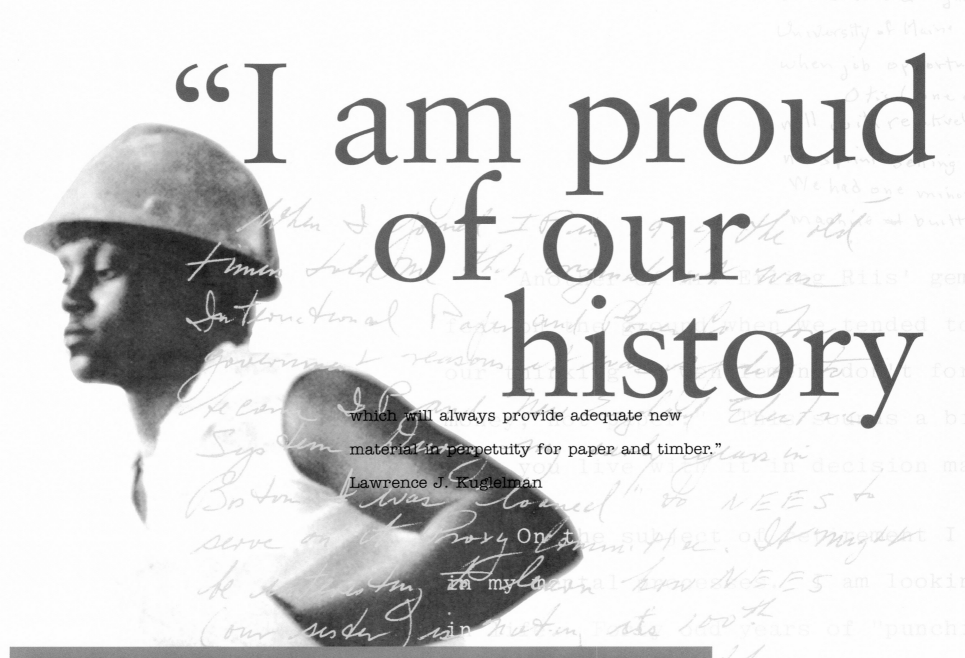

"I am proud of our history

which will always provide adequate new material in perpetuity for paper and timber."
Lawrence J. Kuglelman

"I was the first professional forester hired by International Paper to work as an employee in the New York office—1950. It was a great experience!"

James B. Carlaw

U.S. POSTAGE
PAID
MADISON, FL
32340
MAY 01, '97
AMOUNT

UNITED STATES
POSTAL SERVICE

0000   20151 $1.88
00069923-46

James B Carlaw
6 Camelot Rd
Yarmouth Port MA 02675-1305

The History Factory

International Paper

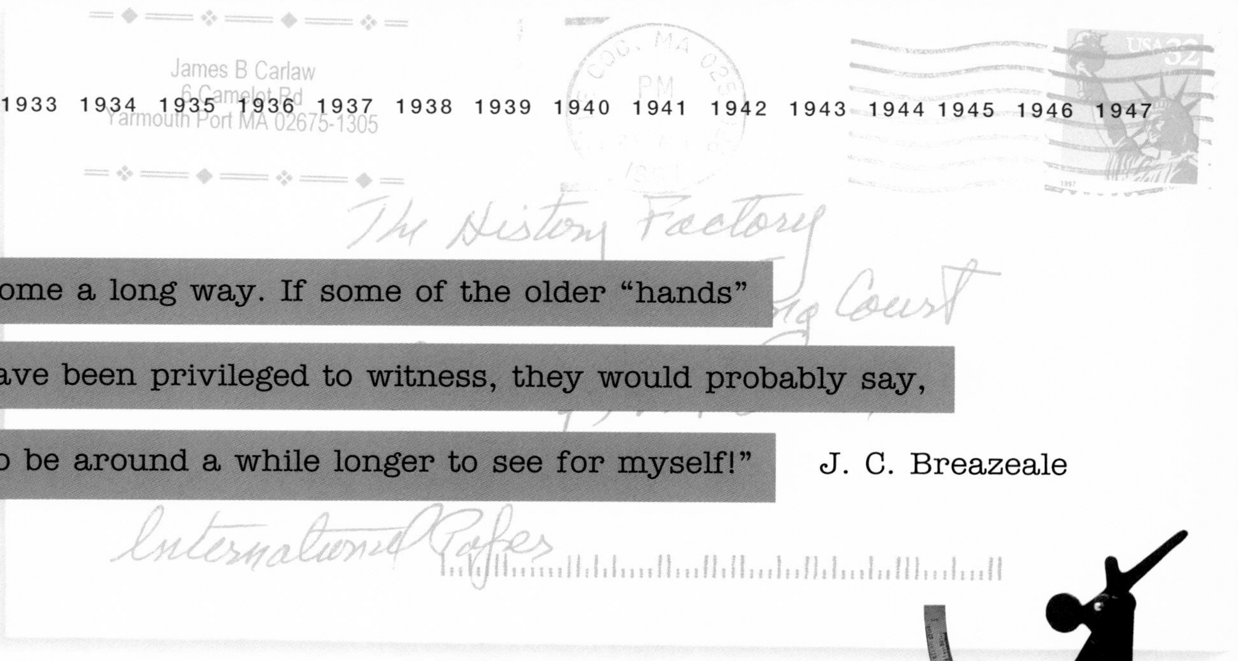

"The paper making business has come a long way. If some of the older "hands" could see the modern innovations which I have been privileged to witness, they would probably say, "What is this industry coming to?" I plan to be around a while longer to see for myself!"

J. C. Breazeale

"International Paper has been a fine big company for a long time, and should be proud to be nearing their 100 year birthday."

John M. Myers

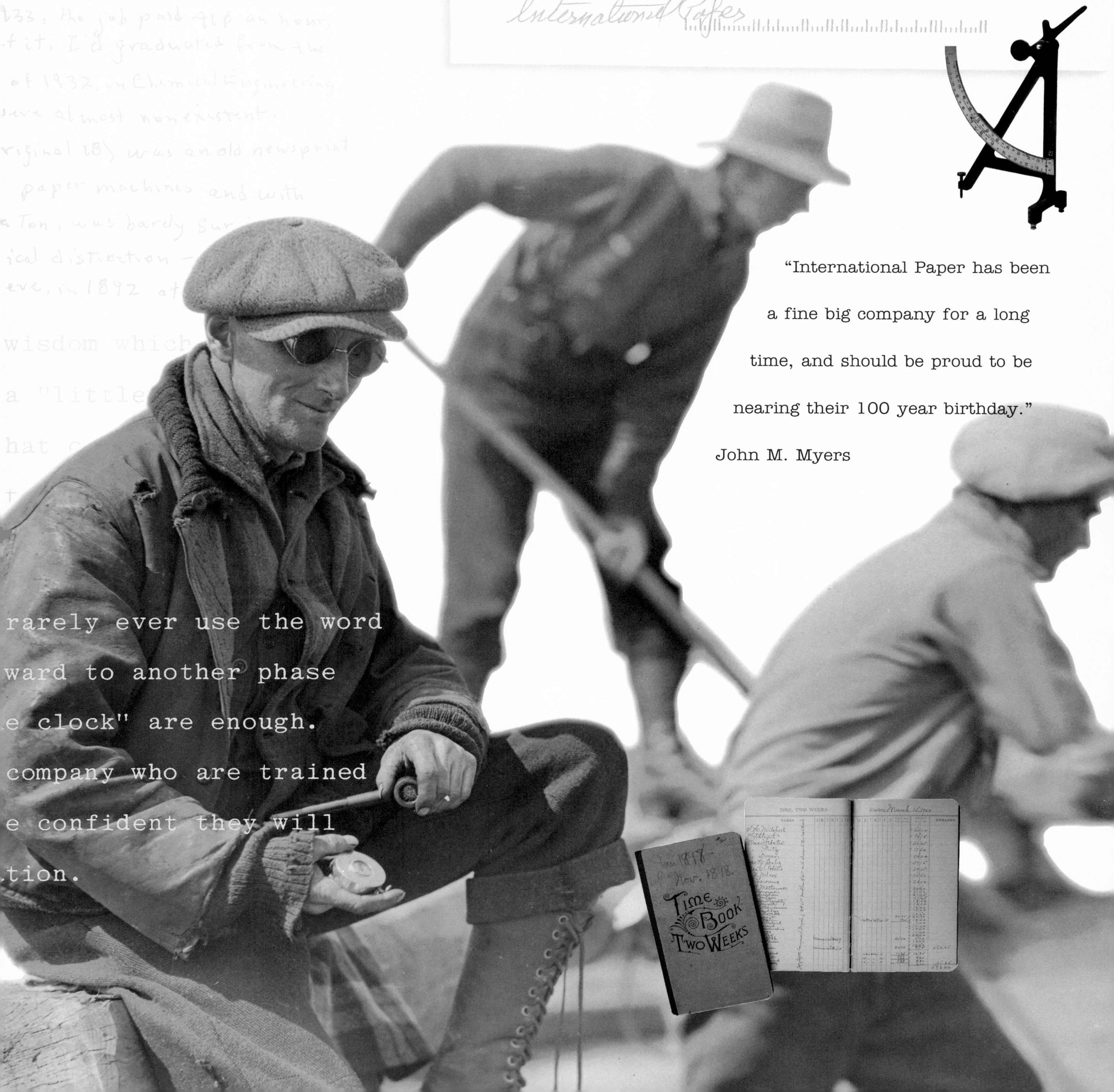

rarely ever use the word

ward to another phase

e clock" are enough.

company who are trained

e confident they will

tion.

June 1878 –
Nov. 1898.

TIME
BOOK
TWO WEEKS

"On a personal basis, I wouldn't mind starting over again with IP Co.

It's a fascinating game and one which captures my imagination as much

today as it did when I started. For a hustler and a doer it offers a tremendous professional

challenge and opportunity."   Minge Reed

"During my active years there was very little movement from one

company to another. As a result many lasting friendships were made.

I credit IP for that."   William W. Morrow

" I loved my job, and I enjoyed working for International Paper Co.

God Bless all of you. Keep up the good work. We were the best."

Josephine Russell

USA 32

"Through the years many loyal employees worked faithfully and hard to

accomplish the goals set up by International Paper. Almost all the employees

contributed to a better life in the communities in which they lived."   A.L. Hughes

"To many of the people of Richmond Hill, International Paper

will always have a warm place in their hearts, and will be ever thankful

for having been part of such a great company." Margaret Fennell Judy

Fold at line over top of envelope to
the right of the return address

CERTIFIED

P 135 319 971

MAIL

GENERATIONS
OF
PRIDE

INTERNATIONAL PAPER FROM A TO Z

GENERATIONS OF PRIDE

INTERNATIONAL PAPER FROM A TO Z

George La Monte and J.H Hall
Figured Writing Paper
February 9, 1875

R.O Lowrey Mode of Water-
proofing Paper Cloth
August 4, 1868

Credit: Courtesy Dennis Thomas
Washington, D.C.

AGAR MANUFACTURING CORPORATION

The Agar Manufacturing Corporation, a leader in corrugated box manufacturing, was the forerunner of International Paper's Container Division.

Alvin Agar founded the company in 1915 and built a small container plant in Brooklyn, New York. Among its first products were Wheaties cereal boxes for the General Mills Company. Box production took a step forward with the introduction of kraft linerboard during the 1920s. Supplied by IP, the nation's leading kraft linerboard producer of the 1930s, Agar Manufacturing enjoyed strong growth and added plants in Somerville, Massachusetts; Whippany, New Jersey; Chicago, Illinois; and Kansas City, Kansas.

International Paper acquired the company in 1940, becoming one of the first integrated paper producers in the industry. Operating under its original name, Agar Manufacturing built a box plant at IP's Georgetown, South Carolina, mill, producing heavy-duty V-Board boxes for shipment of military goods and food rations. In December 1944, its name was changed to International Paper Container Corporation.

AKROSIL

Akrosil's origins date from 1917, when it was founded in Menasha, Wisconsin, as the Edgewater Paper Company. During the early years, Edgewater produced gummed tape and sanitary paper that barbers attached to the headrests of their chairs.

In the 1960s, research scientist Ales M. Kapral developed Edgewater's silicone-coated release paper business. The company installed its first one-station coater in 1967 and two years later was acquired by Kapral, who changed its name to Akrosil, combining his initials and the word silicone. Akrosil worked closely with the Thilmany Pulp and Paper Company, its main supplier of specialty kraft paper.

Flourishing during the 1970s, Akrosil added a research facility, a new office building and a second silicone coater. Soon it branched out into the disposable diaper, automotive, pressure-sensitive tape and sanitary napkin markets.

Shortly after Akrosil was acquired by the Hammermill Paper Company in 1975, it abandoned all non-silicone product lines and was integrated into Thilmany. Along with Hammermill and Thilmany, Akrosil joined the IP family in 1986. During subsequent years, Akrosil expanded into new markets and opened plants in Heerlen, The Netherlands; Lancaster, Ohio; and Toronto, Canada. By the 1990s, Akrosil was an international leader in the silicone-coated release paper and film business.

ANDROSCOGGIN PULP AND PAPER MILL, JAY, MAINE

The Androscoggin mill began operations on the Androscoggin River in Jay, Maine, in 1965. International Paper's first Northern mill to produce bleached kraft pulp, Androscoggin was equipped with a continuous digester that produced 500 tons of high-quality pulp per day. In addition to meeting the mill's own needs, the Androscoggin digester also supplied pulp to the nearby Otis mill in Livermore Falls, and to the Hudson River mill in Corinth, New York. Androscoggin originally operated two paper machines. The No. 1 machine produced lightweight colored bond grades and the No. 2 machine made carbonizing tissue. In 1967, the mill added its No. 3 machine to produce coated publication papers.

From 1975 to 1977, a $175 million expansion program, the largest in the company's history to that date, added two paper machines, a new woodyard, a second continuous pulp digester, a new bleach plant and additions to the power plant. The new No. 4 machine produced lightweight uncoated colored and white grades, and the No. 5 machine made Data-Coat—a lightweight carbonizing tissue. When the demand for carbonizing tissue declined during the 1980s, Androscoggin converted its No. 2 machine to coated grades. In the 1990s, No. 5 machine was converted to specialty papers.

The Androscoggin mill recently completed a major rebuild of its No. 4 machine to produce lightweight coated freesheet publication papers. It has a capacity of 200,000 tons per year, bringing the mill's total capacity to 575,000 tons of paper per year.

Today the mill includes a woodyard, a groundwood mill, a flash dryer producing market pulp, three woodrooms, utilities, two continuous pulp digesters, two bleach plants, five paper machines—each nearly as long as a football field—and deep well storage for finished paper-products. The mill employs more than 1,200 people. Androscoggin's paper is converted to internationally recognized end products such as magazines, catalogs, fast-food wrappers and a variety of specialty and office papers.

Androscoggin mill

ARIZONA CHEMICAL

Launched as a joint venture of International Paper and American Cyanamid in 1930, Arizona Chemical processed by-products of the papermaking processes and became a global leader in pulp chemicals. It started operations in Camp Verde, Arizona, extracting salt cake used in black liquor recovery furnaces that supplied paper mills. However, the project failed and the mine closed in 1933. Starting over in 1937, Arizona Chemical built salt cake plants in Texas at O'Donnell and Brownfield.

Arizona Chemical, Camp Verde, Arizona

Arizona Chemical launched a new line of business after researchers had developed a method to clean crude liquor turpentine. In 1937, in an effort to refine this by-product of the sulfate digester process, the company built a pinene plant at Panama City, Florida, supplying IP's Southern Kraft Division with beta pinene fuel.

Another scientific breakthrough in the 1940s led to the discovery of a technique to derive crude tall oil from black liquor soap. This opened up new product lines, including chemicals used for soaps and surface coatings, as well as sizings and emulsifiers. Arizona Chemical commercialized the tall oil process at the Panama City plant in 1946 and at its new facility at IP's Springhill, Louisiana, mill. Tall oil processing became Arizona Chemical's primary business. The company phased out its O'Donnell and Brownfield operations by the late 1940s, and in the 1950s it added more tall oil

capacity at the Panama City location. It also added a new refining plant at Springhill in 1960 and established its own research laboratory in 1961.

Demand for Arizona Chemical's products skyrocketed in the 1960s as it became a leading supplier for producers of adhesives, sealants and synthetic rubber, triggering another round of plant upgrades during the 1970s.

International Paper acquired full ownership of the company in 1985 and supported its ambitious growth program during subsequent years. In the United States, Arizona Chemical added plants through acquisitions in Pensacola and Port St. Joe, Florida; Oakdale, Louisiana; Picayune, Mississippi; and Gulfport, Mississippi (later closed). Building up its presence in Europe, the company operates chemical facilities at Sandarne, Sweden; Greaker, Norway; Niort, France; and Oulu and Valkeakoski, Finland.

Facility Location	Year built/ acquired
Panama City, Florida	1936
Springhill, Louisiana	1960
Global Office, Panama City, Florida*	1985
Port St. Joe, Florida*	1986
Picayune, Mississippi*	1986
Sandarne, Sweden*	1988
Pensacola, Florida*	1989
Oakdale, Louisiana*	1989
Gulfport, Mississippi #	1989
Greaker, Norway*	1993
Niort, France*	1995
Oulu, Finland*	1996
Valkeakoski, Finland*	1996

*acquired
closed

AUGUSTA, GEORGIA PULP AND PAPER MILL

The Augusta, Georgia, mill was built during the late 1950s by the Robert Gair Company, which had been founded in the late 19th century by the inventor of the folding carton. Before the mill was completed, the Robert Gair Company was acquired by the Continental Can Company, which completed the mill in 1961. Originally designed as a one-machine mill, Augusta installed a second Fourdrinier in 1964 and a third in 1977. Conveniently located in close proximity to extensive woodlands and water supplies, the mill produced mostly bleached sulfate paper-board. Unfortunately, its board production capacity was much larger than its pulp man-ufacturing capacity, requiring extensive pur-chases of market pulp made by other mills.

In 1985, Augusta and other property controlled by Continental Can were acquired for $317 million by the Federal Paper Board Company. Tackling the mill's major problem, Federal shipped large amounts of pulp from its Riegelwood, North Carolina, mill while working on a long-term solution that involved the installation of new pulping capacity. This was part of an eight-year, $1.1 billion modernization program that turned Augusta into the largest solid bleached sulfate paperboard mill in the world (a distinction that previously belonged to Federal's Riegelwood mill) with a daily capacity of 1,745 tons. Its primary product was heavy paperboard used by the packaging industry, including the Imperial Cup Corporation, which was acquired by Federal Paper Board in 1989. In 1996, Federal Paper Board merged with International Paper and the latter integrated Augusta into its paperboard operations.

AUSSEDAT REY

A French producer of pulp, reprographic, specialty and graphic papers, and decorative panels, Aussedat Rey was acquired by International Paper in 1989. Aussedat Rey was formed in 1970 following a merger of the Aussedat Paper Company and the Rey Cellulose and Chemicals Production Company. In 1974, Aussedat Rey acquired Papeteries de France group, which was founded in 1869 by Aristide Bergés. Papeteries de France included 14 mills and a well-known distribution business. Aussedat Rey at that time supplied 10 percent of all copy paper used in continental Europe.

The groundwork for the Aussedat Paper Company was laid in 1788 by Augustin Aussedat, a French papermaker who became manager of a small paper mill in Leysse, in what is today France. In 1806, his son, Alexis Aussedat, took control of a paper mill in Crane that later became Aussedat's main production facility. After the installation of its first paper machine in 1842, the Aussedat Paper Company quickly established itself as a major producer of writing papers. In the 1960s, Aussedat began producing copy papers for the Rank Xerox Corporation and acquired a paper mill at Pont-de-Claix.

Founded in 1871, Rey became France's largest tannin producer, with plants at Saillat and Couzes. It expanded into cellulose production during the 1920s. In the 1940s, Rey expanded its mill at Saillat, which became the largest tannin and pulp producer in post-World War II France.

Beginning in the 1950s, the company specialized in decorative panels (under the Polyrey® brandname) at the Couzes and Ussel facilities, whereas Saillat became a pulp and paper facility.

In 1989, International Paper gained a major presence in Europe when it acquired Aussedat Rey for $1.5 billion.

Aussedat Rey Mill, Saillat, France

BASTROP, LOUISIANA PULP AND PAPER MILL

Designed and built by Richard Cullen, the Bastrop mill in Bastrop, Louisiana, was one of the first mills involved in Southern kraft paper production. It became operational with the start of a sulfite plant in 1921; con-tainerboard manufacturing began two years later. In 1925, International Paper acquired the Bastrop Pulp and Paper Company and integrated the mill into IP's Southern opera-tions. In 1927, IP acquired a second local kraft mill that also had been built by Cullen. Named the Louisiana mill, it worked closely with the Bastrop mill but operated as a sepa-rate facility. The Bastrop mill added a second containerboard machine at the height of a paper boom in 1926. The Great Depression of the 1930s forced the mill to shut down for extended periods of time.

Bastrop staged a comeback during the 1940s when it began manufacturing Chem Fibre®, an innovative corrugating medium developed by IP that was made from 100 percent hardwood pulp. Chem Fibre enabled IP to process Southern hardwoods, which had previously not been considered suitable for paper production. Later improvements increased Bastrop's daily output from 174 to 574 tons.

In the 1970s, as manufacturing equipment for corrugating medium became wider, the mill's narrow paper machines could not compete with newer machines forcing it to shut down in 1982.

Bastrop mill

BODCAW COMPANY

When International Paper acquired the Bodcaw Company of Dallas, Texas, in 1979, it acquired some of the best timberlands in the Southern states, as well as a containerboard mill in Pineville, Louisiana.

Bodcaw traced its origins to the early 1870s, when William Buchanan, a young entrepreneur from Tennessee, founded a sawmill business. In 1889, he acquired the Bodcaw Lumber Company in Stamps, Arkansas, from a group of local businessmen. Along with other sawmills, Buchanan also bought large tracts of timberland as well as oil and gas fields in Louisiana and Arkansas. These various holdings were consolidated into the Bodcaw Company with headquarters in Dallas.

In the 1940s, when many of Bodcaw's timberlands were cleared, the company's new leader, Stanley Seeger, initiated an ambitious reforestation program. This effort yielded some of the region's finest timberlands. In partnership with two European companies, Bodcaw built a kraft mill at Pineville, Louisiana, which turned Bodcaw's timber into linerboard starting in 1968. The mill experienced several renovations during the 1970s, when it added a couch press, new dryers and a modern chip unloading system.

In the late 1970s, when it owned 320,000 acres of timberlands and held the cutting rights on an additional 120,000 acres, Bodcaw received large offers for its valuable holdings from International Paper and the Weyerhaeuser Company. International Paper intended to add the Pineville mill and Bodcaw's extensive timberlands to its assets as part of its capital development program. Waging a bidding war against Weyerhaeuser, IP acquired Bodcaw for $805 million in 1979. International Paper sold the oil and gas businesses and integrated Bodcaw's mill and timberlands into its holdings.

In addition to helping supply the Pineville mill, Bodcaw's timberlands helped provide fiber for IP's new containerboard mill in Mansfield, Louisiana, as well as the company's growing wood products division, including a new plywood and lumber manufacturing plant at Springhill, Louisiana. The Pineville mill became a specialty mill in International Paper's containerboard division and developed products such as Pineliner® high-performance liners, ColorBrite® smooth printing and coating liners for display packaging, and drum liner for fiber drums. Pineville, which had traditionally exported a significant amount of its output, in the 1990s supplied linerboard to U.S. customers and International Paper's container plants.

Bodcaw lumber mill

CAMDEN, ARKANSAS PULP AND PAPER MILL

The Camden mill, the first major pulp and paper mill in the state of Arkansas, was constructed in 1927 and commenced production early the following year. It became one of the Southern Kraft Division's flagship mills. Camden's two paper machines produced unbleached kraft paper, with a daily capacity of 150 tons. A third machine was installed in 1936. The mill initially supplied its product for conversion into bags, but in 1930 Camden added converting operations with a multiwall bag plant (closed in 1997). Other upgrades in the 1930s and 1940s expanded Camden's production to include coated and specialty papers such as file folders and envelopes, and wet-strength products such as Garbax®, a refuse and composting bag.

Camden reached a milestone in 1950, when it installed the first continuous digester in North America, using process technology developed at the Erling Riis Research Laboratory in Mobile, Alabama. The mill expanded its capacity with the installation of a 700-ton Kamyr digester in the 1960s and was among the first to install waste clarifier and black liquor oxidation systems. It also added a computerized paper recycling plant with a daily capacity of 300 tons.

Loading a digester with wood chips.

CANADIAN INTERNATIONAL PAPER

For more than three-quarters of a century, International Paper was the largest producer of Canadian newsprint through its subsidiary, Canadian International Paper (CIP).

When International Paper was formed in 1898, the company produced newsprint at most of its mills in the northeastern United States. In 1913, however, Congress removed tariffs on imported Canadian newsprint, and the American market was flooded with inexpensive imports. Finding it difficult to compete with low-cost producers north of the border, IP chose to expand into Canada.

The foundations for CIP were laid in 1916, when an IP subsidiary named St. Maurice Valley Lumber Company was incorporated in Quebec. In 1922, St. Maurice built its first Canadian newsprint mill at Three Rivers, Quebec. In 1925, International Paper acquired the Riordon Paper Company, Ltd., a bankrupt Canadian pulp and paper producer with mills in Temiskaming, Quebec, and Hawkesbury, Ontario. It integrated these holdings into the St. Maurice Lumber Company and renamed the new organization Canadian International Paper (CIP).

Thriving on inexpensive Canadian timber supplies, CIP built newsprint mills at Gatineau, Quebec, and Dalhousie, New Brunswick. Research and development were centralized at a laboratory in Hawkesbury, which specialized in wood cellulose research. In 1954, CIP acquired a kraft mill at La Tuque, Quebec, that produced pulp, board and paper. It also entered the converting field by branching out into container production.

The North American newsprint industry entered a period of decline during the 1970s as a result of slack demand and overcapacity. In 1981, International Paper sold CIP for $900 million, reinvesting the money into a modernization of its manufacturing operations in the United States.

CARTER HOLT HARVEY, LTD.

In 1995, International Paper acquired majority shareholder status of New Zealand-based Carter Holt Harvey, Ltd., a leading international forest and wood products company. IP acquired a small percentage of Carter Holt Harvey's shares in 1991. In the course of the next four years, IP increased its ownership in Carter Holt Harvey, to just over 50 percent.

Beginning in the latter part of the 19th century, members of the Carter family gradually built up a sawmilling business comprised of seven sawmills and three retail yards in New Zealand. Under the leadership of K.C.A. Carter, the Carter holdings were reorganized in 1951 into a public company, Carter Consolidated, Ltd., with headquarters in Auckland, which opened the way for radiata pine in the market. In 1971, it merged with the Robert Holt & Sons, Ltd., a trading company whose origins dated back to the late 1850s, and subsequently expanded into pulp production.

As one of New Zealand's leading industrial employers during the 1970s, Carter Holt Harvey was a vertically integrated business with strongholds in timber, building supplies, pulp and transportation. It had a number of

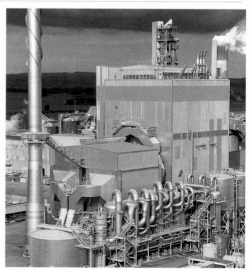

Carter Holt Harvey mill

successful joint ventures with New Zealand companies, including the acquisition in 1985 of a leading public company, Alex Harvey Industries, Ltd., and the subsequent formation of the present Carter Holt Harvey, Ltd. Several years later, Carter Holt Harvey acquired the New Zealand tissue manufacturer Caxton and a major share of the Chilean conglomerate Copec, with extensive holdings in the fuel and forestry sectors.

In the 1990s, Carter Holt Harvey expanded even further with the purchase of state-owned radiata pine forest assets and the acquisition of the large New Zealand forest-based company, Elders Resources NZFP, Ltd. These ambitious acquisitions left Carter Holt Harvey with a weakened balance sheet, precipitating a major restructuring. David Oskin, a corporate officer of International Paper, was named chief executive officer of Carter Holt Harvey. Oskin refocused Carter Holt Harvey on its core business in forest products, improved its financial performance and reduced its long-term indebtedness.

CINCINNATI TECHNOLOGY CENTER

Located in Loveland, Ohio, near Cincinnati, International Paper's Cincinnati Technology Center includes the Packaging Development Center and the Manufacturing Technology Center.

Completed in 1996, the PDC is a 182,500-square-foot complex that consolidated the operations of six other IP facilities, including laboratories and offices, that had been located throughout the eastern United States. The major components transferred to the new center included the Packaging Innovation Center in Middletown, New York; the aseptic product development group in Raleigh, North Carolina; packaging materials engineering and analytical sciences from the Erling Riis Research Laboratory in Mobile, Alabama; the graphic arts group from the Corporate Research Center in Sterling Forest, New York; and the folding carton product development group in Cincinnati, Ohio. In addition to office space, laboratories and training facilities, the PDC features several major pilot project plants for development work in flexographic printing, aseptic packaging and extrusion coating technology. The center is designed so that ideas can move quickly from conception to the laboratory stage to pilot plant trials.

IP announced in 1996 that it would close its engineering and manufacturing services offices in Mobile, Alabama, and relocate the groups to a new building in Loveland. The 120,000-square-foot Manufacturing Technology Center (MTC) is connected to the PDC via an enclosed pedestrian bridge.

The MTC incorporates the computer and communication technology that permits faster problem solving and provides the data, voice and video links required to compete in a global economy. The building also includes training facilities used to improve the manufacturing skills of employees throughout the company. In addition to housing part of International Paper's technology organization, the MTC includes corporate purchasing, liquid packaging engineering and the company's human resources Midwest Regional Resource Center. The MTC opened in June 1997.

CHIEF EXECUTIVE OFFICERS

HUGH CHISHOLM

Hugh Chisholm (1847-1912), one of International Paper's founders, served as the company's president from 1898 to 1907.

Born in Canada, Chisholm began his career as a newsboy on trains running between Toronto and Detroit. Possessing considerable business acumen, he soon controlled newspaper distribution on major Canadian and U.S. railroads and steamboats. In 1865, he sold the business to his brothers, emigrated to the United States and became an American citizen.

As a newspaper dealer and owner of a publishing house in Portland, Maine, Chisholm became interested in the paper business. After an exhaustive study of industry conditions, he acquired a small mill in Livermore, Maine, and organized the Umbagog Pulp Company in 1881. By 1885, Umbagog operated two paper machines. Two years later, Chisholm organized the Otis Falls Pulp Company, which was

followed by another venture that led to the formation of an extensive paper mill and power complex at Rumford, Maine, in 1891.

Believing that a large-scale merger of major American paper companies would stabilize the industry, Chisholm joined William Russell, A. N. Burbank and other industry leaders to form International Paper. After years of negotiations and exhaustive studies, a merger agreement for the International Paper Company was formalized on January 31, 1898, at Albany, New York. At the company's first board meeting, William Russell was elected president but he died in less than six months. Hugh Chisholm, who had been elected first vice president, then became president of the new enterprise which was the world's largest paper company.

Widely considered the most powerful man of the time in the American pulp and paper industry, Chisholm helped IP gain control of 60 percent of the American newsprint market.

His skillful financial management enabled the company to post significant profits throughout the early years. Chisholm's success raised the ire of newspaper owners who argued that the "paper trust" charged exorbitant prices for newsprint. Chisholm denied these accusations at several highly publicized Congressional hearings.

During his tenure at the helm of the company, Chisholm initiated IP's first forest management programs. In 1901, he issued instructions forbidding the harvest of immature trees. He also forged a close relationship with Yale University's forestry program, whose faculty and students helped IP select trees for cutting.

In 1907, Chisholm resigned as IP president so that he could devote his efforts to developing the Oxford Paper Company at Rumford Falls, Maine. He was succeeded by A. N. Burbank.

A.N. BURBANK

A former paper mill owner and one of IP's founders in 1898, Burbank was elected president of the company in 1907, succeeding Hugh Chisholm.

Throughout his tenure, Burbank was confronted with a business recession that affected International Paper's earnings, forcing him to reduce dividends and wages.

Continuing his predecessor's commitment to responsible forestry, Burbank formulated a policy statement on modern woodlands management that was adopted by the board of directors in 1908. He also supported the establishment of IP's first tree nursery in Vermont.

Burbank stepped down as president in 1913 to be succeeded by Philip Dodge.

Philip Dodge (1851-1931) served as president of International Paper from 1913 to 1924.

Born in Fond du Lac, Wisconsin, Dodge attended George Washington University Law School. He joined his father's law practice in 1873 and became an attorney for the Remington Typewriter Company. He became interested in mechanized typesetting and served as a patent expert and legal advisor for the Mergenthaler Printing Company. In 1891, Mergenthaler's board of directors elected Dodge president.

Due to his familiarity with the printing industry, Dodge was elected president of IP in 1913. Soon afterward, he guided International Paper through a major challenge when Congress lifted tariffs on cheaper Canadian newsprint, resulting in a loss of significant market share by IP mills operating in the Northeast. In his first report to IP stockholders, Dodge laid out a comprehensive agenda to tackle these problems. To become more competitive and profitable, International Paper had to build its own newsprint mills in Canada—where pulpwood was far less expensive—and to convert its American mills to other products.

Dodge's efforts to implement this strategy were sidetracked by World War I as International Paper struggled with short-ages of manpower, raw materials and waterpower. In the early 1920s, still committed to his plan to explore new business opportunities for IP in Canada, Dodge raised money for the construction of the company's first Canadian newsprint mill at Three Rivers, Quebec. The giant plant was completed in 1922 and later became the world's largest newsprint mill. In the United States, Dodge initiated the development of hydroelectric power plants near IP mills in Glens Falls, New York, and Berlin, New Hampshire.

Dodge retired as International Paper president in 1924. He was succeeded by Archibald Graustein, who continued to pursue major elements of Dodge's agenda.

As president from 1924 to 1936, Archibald Graustein expanded IP and steered the company during the early years of the Great Depression.

Graustein (1885-1969) graduated from Harvard Law School in 1907 and became a prominent member of the corporate law firm Ropes, Gray & Gorham in Boston. During the early 1920s, he gained recognition for his role in the reorganization of the bankrupt Riordon Paper Company, a Canadian firm later acquired by International Paper.

When International Paper's board of directors elected Graustein president in 1924, the company was in dire straits. Its aging Northeastern mills were in no posi-tion to compete with modern Canadian plants, which supplied the bulk of newsprint consumed in the United States. Building on initiatives started by his predecessor, Philip Dodge, Graustein devised a multi-faceted strategy to tackle IP's problems. First, he converted most older facilities from newsprint to more profitable specialty grades, which ensured the survival of IP's Northeastern mills. Second, he engineered IP's expansion into Canada with the acquisition of the Riordon properties, which were reorganized as part of Canadian International Paper in 1925. This move enabled IP to maintain its viability as the world's leading newsprint manufacturer. Third, in 1925, Graustein negotiated the acquisition of the Bastrop Pulp and Paper Company, a pioneer of Southern paper production that later became part of the Southern Kraft Division. To increase kraft production, Graustein advocated the construction of major Southern kraft mills such as Camden, Arkansas; Mobile, Alabama; and Panama City, Florida.

As part of his reorganization strategy, Graustein built up IP's presence in hydroelectric power production in the Northeastern states and Canada. This strategy backfired in 1935, however, when Congress passed the Public Utility Holdings Act that outlawed the combination of manufacturing operations with power production.

The mill conversion program and the buildup of Canadian International Paper, the Southern Kraft Division and IP's hydroelectric power business significantly increased the company's debts during the late 1920s. Graustein's plans to retire the $330 million debt in orderly fashion were shattered by the Great Depression, which triggered an unprecedented decline in the pulp and paper business. Blamed for IP's precarious financial condition, Graustein resigned in 1936. He was succeeded by Richard Cullen. Graustein subsequently opened a private law practice in New York City.

RICHARD J. CULLEN

A pioneer of the American pulp and paper industry, Richard Cullen (1866-1948) served as International Paper's president and chairman during a critical period in the 1930s and 1940s.

Born in Canada, Cullen worked as a mechanical engineer for the Riordon Paper Company, a leading pulp producer that later became part of Canadian International Paper. In 1898, he designed and supervised the construction of Riordon's Hawkesbury mill in Ontario, one of Canada's first sulfite pulp mills. He emigrated to the United States in 1909 to serve as manager of the Cushnoc Paper Company in Augusta, Maine.

Cullen played a key role in the development of kraft pulp and paper production in the South, which traditionally had not been a papermaking region because of difficulties processing its tree species. He organized the Bastrop Pulp and Paper Company and designed a kraft mill at Bastrop, Louisiana. Built under Cullen's supervision in 1920, the Bastrop mill featured innovative kraft technology that enabled it to utilize Southern pine for pulp and paper.

In 1924, Cullen built a second facility, the Louisiana mill, also located in Bastrop. Lacking sufficient financial resources to realize his grand vision of

building up the Southern paper industry, however, Cullen decided to team with International Paper. The giant paper company, which was in the midst of a major expansion at the time, acquired Cullen's Bastrop mill in 1925, followed by the Louisiana mill two years later. Cullen joined IP in 1927 as a vice president. As president of the Southern International Paper Company (a predecessor of the Southern Kraft Division), Cullen built up the company's base in the South through the construction of kraft mills at Camden, Arkansas; Mobile, Alabama; Panama City, Florida; Georgetown, South Carolina; and Springhill, Louisiana. Cullen also helped negotiate the acquisition of the Moss Point, Mississippi, mill in 1928.

A gifted engineer, Cullen initiated IP's efforts to use Fourdrinier machines to produce kraft board for shipping containers. International Paper's mill at Panama City, Florida, became the first American mill to produce kraft linerboard on the Fourdrinier machine.

In 1936, Cullen became International Paper's president, replacing Archibald Graustein, who had resigned the position. He inherited a company in deep financial trouble. Cullen reinvigorated International Paper by dissolving or selling off poorly performing subsidiaries and by recapitalizing the company. He phased out IP's hydroelectric power operations to comply with the Public Utility Holdings Act of 1935, which outlawed the combination of manufacturing operations and commercial power production.

As IP president, Cullen also initiated several investments in new technologies that enabled the company to generate profitable products, such as the successful effort to manufacture kraft linerboard on the Fourdrinier machine. The company also sharply expanded its corrugated container output and increased its raw materials base in the South through the acquisition of large tracts of timberland.

In 1943, Cullen was succeeded as president by John Hinman and moved to the newly created post of chairman of the corporation.

JOHN H. HINMAN

Described by the press as "the man who ran IP with an iron hand," John Hinman (1885-1981) served as president and chairman of the board during the 1940s and 1950s, when the company enjoyed unprecedented prosperity.

Born in North Stratford, New Hampshire, Hinman joined International Paper in 1913 as a woodlands manager of the American Realty Company, an IP subsidiary. A passionate forester, he was committed to the conservation of the company's timberlands and launched massive reforestation programs. He was appointed general manager of IP's timberland and woods operations in 1927 and in the following year became vice president of the company. In the late 1930s, Hinman served as president of Canadian International Paper, IP's main subsidiary at the time, and in 1943 succeeded Richard Cullen as president of IP.

At the beginning of his presidency, Hinman completed the financial recovery initiated by his predecessor. By the late 1940s, the company was virtually debt free. Hinman vastly expanded IP's landholdings, more than doubling the company's fee-owned lands from 2.5 million to 5.8 million acres. To enhance forest management and research, he developed IP's professional forestry services and supported the SuperTree™ research program and scientific work aimed at a fuller use of forest resources. An early advocate of corporate responsibility, Hinman was instrumental in establishing the International Paper Company Foundation, which supported public education.

In 1954, Hinman was succeeded as president by Richard Doane but continued to lead the company as chairman of the board. His determination to turn IP into a diversified forest products company culminated in 1956 with the acquisition of the Long-Bell Lumber Corporation. Long-Bell's vast assets included 450,000 acres of timberland, sawmills, manufacturing plants and wholesale and retail distribution networks, comprising the world's largest lumber company. Hinman defended the Long-Bell acquisition against the Federal Trade Commission, which claimed that the $117 million transaction violated anti-trust laws. Other important acquisitions of the Hinman era included the A. M. Collins Manufacturing Company and the Lord Baltimore Press, which produced folding cartons.

Hinman was succeeded as chairman of the board by Richard Doane in 1961.

RICHARD C. DOANE

Richard C. Doane (1898-1972) led International Paper during the late 1950s and early 1960s as chairman of the board, president and chief executive officer.

A Philadelphia native, Doane graduated from Yale in 1919. He joined International Paper in 1924 as a sales manager, specializing in newsprint sales. In 1929, he became vice president of the IP Sales Company, then the company's newsprint marketing division. In 1938, Doane transferred to the IP Sales Company's Montreal office and became its president in 1941. Rejoining IP's New York headquarters in 1948, he became vice president and general sales manager. In 1954, Doane became president of International Paper, succeeding John Hinman, who retained his position as chairman of the board. Doane was named chief executive officer in 1959. He helped establish the Overseas Division which vastly expanded IP's export business.

Elected chairman of IP's board in 1961, Doane strengthened the corrugated container business and supported the

introduction of computer technology at the Georgetown, South Carolina, mill in 1962. Extending IP's reach to the West Coast, Doane mobilized investments for

International Paper's new linerboard mill at Gardiner, Oregon.

Doane retired as chairman of the board in 1966.

EDWARD B. HINMAN

The son of John Hinman, a major figure in the history of International Paper, Edward B. Hinman served as president and chief executive officer in the late 1960s.

Hinman (b. 1914) joined Canadian International Paper as a laborer at the Gatineau mill in Quebec, Canada. Rising through the ranks of Canadian International Paper, IP's newsprint subsidiary, he was elected vice president of IP in 1965. One year later, he became president and chief executive officer.

Hinman's tenure coincided with a difficult period in the company's history. Virtually debt-free and in control of valuable assets, the company was a tempting target for a hostile takeover. Moreover, IP had to shore up its position in U.S. markets, where it had lost a signif-

icant share during the 1960s. Hinman tried to solve these problems by borrowing large sums for an ambitious diversification strategy into consumer products, medical products, real estate and construction. He also initiated a $1 billion program to increase International Paper's production capacity by 25 percent.

By the end of 1969, Hinman had increased IP's debt-to-equity ratio from zero to 40 percent, averting a possible takeover. He also supported the development of new business, such as disposable diapers, facial tissues and paper towels. Like many companies that diversified during the late 1960s, IP found the new

markets difficult to enter. Much of the new business, notably diapers, proved unprofitable and had to be abandoned. Meanwhile, demand for newsprint, linerboard and other traditional IP products stagnated, leaving the company with excess capacity. One of the few bright spots was IP's Long-Bell division, which profited from a jump in demand for plywood.

In an attempt to turn the tide, Hinman recruited Frederick R. Kappel, a former chairman of AT&T who was named chairman of IP in 1969. The Kappel-Hinman team continued until 1971, when Hinman retired from the company.

FREDERICK R. KAPPEL

Frederick R. Kappel was chairman of International Paper's board of directors from 1969 to 1971.

A native Minnesotan, Kappel was trained as an engineer and worked as a "ground man" for the Northwestern Bell Company. Rising through the ranks of the telecommunications industry, he served as chairman of American Telephone & Telegraph from 1961 to 1967. Elected International Paper's chairman in February 1969, he was the first leader of the company since Philip Dodge (1912-1924) who had spent most of his career with other firms.

Kappel's short term coincided with a difficult phase in the company's history. Many acquisitions that had been made by his predecessor, Edward Hinman, did not fit into IP's core business. Moreover, demand for pulp and paper stagnated in the late 1960s, just after IP had added major new production capacity with the completion of new mills in Jay, Maine; Gardiner, Oregon: and Vicksburg,

Mississippi. As a result of these and other problems, IP determined that it needed outside help to tackle the challenges of a new era.

Kappel's most important task was to recruit new senior managers who rebuilt the company during subsequent years, including several former AT&T executives. During his term, IP completed its new Corporate Research Center in

Sterling Forest, New York, which strengthened IP's core business by developing new products and process technologies. The company also launched a four-year, $100 million air and water protection program. As part of his plan to reinvigorate senior management, Kappel recruited Paul Gorman, a former AT&T manufacturing executive. Gorman succeeded Kappel in 1971.

PAUL A. GORMAN

As IP chairman during the early 1970s, Paul A. Gorman consolidated the company.

Gorman (1907-1996) spent much of his career at AT&T. In 1969, he was recruited to save the troubled Penn Central Transportation Company but soon decided that it was beyond repair. In 1971, he was recruited by IP chairman Frederick Kappel—a former chairman of AT&T—to succeed him.

International Paper faced serious financial and organizational problems,

including aging facilities, acquisitions that did not fit into its core business and reduced earnings. Gorman launched a program to sell off IP's under-performing acquisitions, including its home-building and medical products subsidiaries. He also closed outdated production facilities in York Haven, Pennsylvania; Italy; Ecuador; West Germany; and Puerto Rico. Believing that IP should pay greater attention to the profitability of its core business operations, Gorman created profit centers that made it easier to monitor their performance. Gorman also

established a rule requiring that any project involving capital spending must be reviewed at all levels and must show a minimum after-tax investment return of 10 percent. His efforts paid off as early as 1972, when IP's profits jumped 30 percent. At the same time, however, his initiatives also significantly expanded the ranks of IP's managerial force, especially at its corporate headquarters in New York City.

Gorman retired as chairman in 1974. He was succeeded by J. Stanford Smith.

J. STANFORD SMITH

As chairman and CEO from 1974 to 1980, J. Stanford Smith (1915-1983) implemented a large-scale reorganization of the company and improved its marketing operations.

Smith graduated from DePauw University and began a successful career at General Electric. He ran GE's computer operations during the late 1960s and later became one of that company's top executives. He joined International Paper in 1973 as vice chairman of the board of directors, and the following year succeeded Paul Gorman as chairman and CEO.

Smith continued his predecessor's program of internal restructuring and consolidation. Convinced that IP could improve its profitability by making better use of its vast timber resources and landholdings, Smith expanded the wood products division and acquired the General Crude Oil Company to explore petroleum and minerals on IP lands.

Using GE's organizational chart as a model, Smith launched a massive restructuring program that replaced the company's geographically-based Southern Kraft Division and Northern Division with a system of functional business units. At a historic meeting in New York in 1976, Smith announced the formation of

the consumer packaging, industrial packaging, specialty packaging, white papers, and wood products and resources units.

Smith launched a series of initiatives to reconfigure IP's aging operations. This resulted in the selling of the Panama City, Florida, mill and the Otis mill in Livermore Falls, Maine, and the shutdown of the Springhill, Louisiana, mill. Other mills, notably the Androscoggin mill at Jay, Maine, were expanded or renovated to improve their cost structure and product mix. Smith also initiated the construction

of a linerboard mill at Mansfield, Louisiana, IP's first new paper mill in more than a decade. Under his leadership, IP acquired the Bodcaw Company, with its large woodland holdings and a paper mill at Pineville, Louisiana, in 1979.

Among Smith's achievements was the establishment of a strong management development process within the company. Smith was succeeded by Edwin A. Gee as CEO in 1979 and as chairman of the board a year later.

EDWIN A. GEE

As International Paper president and chairman during the late 1970s and early 1980s, Edwin A. Gee (b. 1921) initiated a large-scale overhaul of the company's production facilities.

After earning a doctorate in chemical engineering, Gee joined the DuPont Company, where he spent much of his career. In 1978, he was elected president of International Paper, and two years later became chairman of its board of directors.

Gee oversaw a systematic effort to improve IP's manufacturing operations and to make it the paper and pulp industry's leading low-cost producer of high-quality products. To mobilize financial resources for this capital expenditure program, Gee ordered a liquidation of major assets. In 1979, IP sold a $763 million interest in the General Crude Oil Company. Two years later, Canadian

International Paper, an IP subsidiary, was sold for $900 million. Proceeds from these and other transactions financed such projects as the reconfiguration of the Mobile, Alabama, mill from kraft paper and newsprint to uncoated white papers and printing grades. It also financed the conversion of the Georgetown, South Carolina, mill from linerboard production to the manufacture of pulp and bleached paper products such as envelope, bond and copy paper. Half a billion dollars was used to upgrade conversion and distribution operations in IP's wood products business, increasing lumber and plywood production by more than 50 percent. Gee's capital expenditure program—the total cost of which exceeded $6 billion—

lowered IP's production costs by 11 percent from 1981 to 1987.

Drawing upon his experience at DuPont, whose rate of lost-time injuries per million hours worked was .23, Gee also initiated a series of workplace safety programs at IP. Although IP's rate of lost-time injuries at 9.0 was good by paper industry standards, Gee committed the company to achieving a significant reduction. Improved safety training programs and greater attention to accident prevention helped lower IP's rate of lost-time injuries to 2.5 per million work hours within seven years.

Gee was succeeded by John A. Georges as president in 1981 and as CEO in 1984. He remained chairman of the board until 1985.

JOHN A. GEORGES

As chief executive officer of International Paper from 1984 to 1996, John A. Georges directed the globalization of the company.

As chief executive officer of International Paper from 1984 to 1996, Georges transformed the company from a $5 billion business to a global enterprise with sales of nearly $20 billion, 30 percent of which were from international operations.

Georges (b. 1931) received a bachelor's degree in chemical engineering from the University of Illinois and a master's degree in business administration from Drexel University. In 1951, he began a career at DuPont where he served in a variety of senior positions. He joined International Paper in 1979 and was named president and chief operating officer two years later. He succeeded Edwin A. Gee as chief executive officer in 1984 and as chairman of the board in 1985.

Georges continued the modernization and streamlining of the company's core pulp and paper business that had begun under his predecessor. He oversaw the completion of a $6 billion capital investment program that included the reconfiguration of mills in Georgetown, South Carolina, and Mobile, Alabama, as well as major expansions at the Mansfield, Louisiana, facility and the Riverdale mill at Selma, Alabama.

A dynamic leader, Georges designed and implemented an aggressive program of acquisitions in the United States and worldwide. In 1986, he engineered the

$1.1 billion acquisition of the Hammermill Paper Company. The acquisition of this leading producer of printing and writing papers, which included the prestigious Strathmore and Beckett lines of artists' papers and specialty grades, complemented International Paper's strong position in commodity markets.

In 1995, Georges initiated International Paper's merger with Federal Paper Board, a $3.5 billion transaction that was completed the following year. The merger brought a million acres of prime timberland as well as two world-class pulp and paper mills that made International Paper the world's leading producer of bleached board for folding cartons and other packaging applications.

Georges' vision included a leadership position for International Paper in the global pulp, paper and forest products industry. During his tenure, the company acquired Aussedat Rey, a major French paper producer, and Zanders Feinpapiere AG, a leading German manufacturer of top-quality coated grades.

In the Pacific Rim, International Paper acquired a majority position in Carter Holt Harvey, a New Zealand-based forest products company with operations in Australia and South America. In eastern Europe, Georges provided strategic guidance for the 1992 acquisition of the Kwidzyn paper mill near Gdansk, Poland. Kwidzyn implemented a major expansion program and serves a variety of growing markets in eastern and western Europe.

Georges also revamped International Paper's collective bargaining process. In 1984, the company reached an agreement with union officials to phase out the multi-mill contract system in its Southern mills, thus assuring the continued operating future of mills in Camden, Arkansas, and Moss Point and Natchez, Mississippi.

International Paper became an industry leader in employee safety and health during Georges' tenure, reducing recordable injuries by 70 percent between 1988 and 1996. Georges also provided the impetus for company facilities to qualify for the Occupational Safety and Health Administration's Voluntary Protection Program, which recognizes outstanding safety performance throughout American industry. In 1996, International Paper led the nation with 21 facilities either in the federal VPP program or recommended and awaiting official OSHA approval.

Georges was the guiding force behind the company's substantial accomplishments in managing change. His approach was to set seemingly impossible targets and motivate employees to perform beyond them. Georges retired as chairman and chief executive officer in 1996 but remained a member of the board of directors. He was succeeded by John T. Dillon.

JOHN T. DILLON

John Dillon was named chairman and chief executive officer of International Paper in 1996.

Born in 1938, John Dillon started his career with International Paper in 1965 as a sales trainee and subsequently held positions in sales, marketing, planning and general management in most of the company's major business sectors. In 1982, he was elected vice president and group executive for the Land and Timber Group and later assumed additional responsibilities for wood products operations. In 1987 he became executive vice president for the company's Packaging sector and was elected to International Paper's board of directors in 1991.

He holds a bachelor's degree from the University of Hartford and a masters degree from Columbia University's Graduate School of Business.

Dillon served as the company's president and chief operating officer from September 1995 to April 1996, when he was elected chairman and chief executive officer. He was the first CEO in several generations who had spent his entire career with the company.

During the tenure of his predecessor, John Georges, Dillon played a key role in expanding the company's international operations. While serving as executive vice president - packaging, Dillon was responsible for the company's industrial and consumer packaging businesses, as well as its corporate engineering and technology staffs. He was also in charge of the company's operations in Asia and served on the board of directors of Carter Holt Harvey, a New Zealand-based paper and forest products company.

In the early 1980s, as vice president and group executive for the Land and Timber group, Dillon was instrumental in the creation of IP Timberlands, a limited partnership controlled by International Paper. IPT enabled the company to establish a better market value for its undervalued timber holdings and also enhanced the company's ability to manage and finance its more than six million acres of woodlands.

As chairman and chief executive officer of International Paper, one of Dillon's first priorities was to ensure the successful integration of Federal Paper Board, which merged with IP in March 1996 in a $3.5 billion transaction. Year-end results showed the merger ahead of its financial targets, while reinforcing and complementing the product lines of the two entities. In addition, the company completed one of the largest internal expansion programs in its nearly 100-year history and was positioned for market leadership in the next century. In 1996, the trade journal, *Papermaking*, named International Paper its Company of the Year.

Under Dillon's direction, International Paper undertook a thorough evaluation of its businesses leading to decisions that would guide the allocation of capital and set new requirements for acceptable levels of profitability and industry leadership for each business. As a result of this analysis, the company announced in mid-1977 a performance improvement plan that would include the sale of $1 billion in assets.

Dillon also set forth plans for the corporation to be more shareholder-oriented and stated a goal of working toward a 12 percent average return on investment over a business cycle. As part of this objective, each business became responsible for setting its return-on-investment objectives and was held accountable for its results.

In his 1996 letter to shareholders, Dillon stated a goal for International Paper to become the supplier of choice for its customers by offering a total value of products and services that surpass the competition. Included in this initiative were quality assurance and product innovation through technology. A key element in serving customers is Dillon's emphasis on High Performance Organizations, through which employees in all areas of the company have increased decision-making authority and accountability in their jobs.

While competing globally, International Paper and its leadership are guided by the values of the small communities and rural areas that are home to many of the company's operations. In 1996, when there had been a series of arson attacks on rural, largely African American churches, Dillon — working with the National Council of Churches — made the commitment that International Paper would donate and deliver building materials to help the congregations rebuild. Dillon was honored as ABC-TV *World News Tonight's* Person of the Week for his actions.

Under Dillon's leadership, the company developed the International

Paper Agenda, a vision and set of values and goals for the corporation. In 1997, the agenda was translated into 15 languages and distributed to all employees of the company, worldwide. Among the principles of excellence set forth in the agenda are to:

- Develop strategies that differentiate us from our competitors.
- Pursue quality in everything we do.
- Employ the best people and provide the support necessary for them to learn, grow and contribute throughout their careers.
- Believe in the power of teamwork and communication.
- Value diversity and treat each other with dignity and respect.
- Respect and protect the environment, and the health and safety of our fellow employees.
- Manage our natural resources responsibly.
- Be good citizens who actively participate in our communities.
- Be accountable in all that we do.

Commenting to shareholders on the priorities and future direction of International Paper, Dillon said: "You will see from our company more accountability from our businesses for increasing returns on investment, more emphasis on serving customers and greater participation by employees."

COATED PAPERS

Coated paper is printing paper with a surface coated with layers of clay mixed with adhesives and other substances to enhance its finish characteristics. A slick, high-gloss finish is put on the sheet through a process called supercalendering. First introduced in the United States in 1852, coated papers are used mainly for high-gloss printing materials such as magazines, catalogues and newspaper inserts. Magazine-grade coated paper continues to be a profitable, high-value product.

International Paper's Hudson River mill at Corinth, New York, made the company's first coated printing paper in 1946. The addition of the No. 3 machine at the Androscoggin mill in Jay, Maine, in 1968 expanded the company's coated paper business. In the 1980s, IP upgraded its production facilities at both mills, and converted a paper machine at its mill in Pine Bluff, Arkansas, to significantly increase its output of coated paper grades. IP also produced coated papers at the Moss Point, Mississippi, mill, at Aussedat Rey's Anould mill in France, and in Germany, where it acquired a controlling interest in Zanders Feinpapiere AG, a producer of premium coated papers.

CORPORATE RESEARCH CENTER

IP's Corporate Research Center (CRC) in Sterling Forest, New York, continues the company's tradition of laboratory work begun in 1901 with the establishment of the Central Test Bureau in Glens Falls, New York.

Completed in 1969, CRC included the paper and technology group, analytical staff and support personnel from the Glens Falls facility, which was closed. To support coating research and development, CRC operated a large pilot coating plant. During the 1970s, a research group from Canadian International Paper's Hawkesbury, Ontario, laboratory was transferred to CRC to conduct dissolving pulp research and development focusing on viscose rayon. CRC's pulp and bleaching group was staffed by personnel transferred from Hawkesbury and the Erling Riis Research Laboratory in Mobile, Alabama. A pilot pulping plant was added in 1975. CRC also operated a pilot plant to support IP's nonwoven fabrics group, which included hospital supplies. As a result, CRC conducted health and medical research until the early 1980s, when IP sold its hospital supply operations.

During the late 1970s, CRC became active in forest and environmental protection science and expanded this activity during subsequent years. During the 1980s, the center supported the conversion of many IP mills from acid to alkaline papermaking and later developed de-inking technology that enabled the company to use more recovered fiber as a raw material.

Packaging research started in the 1970s and by the early 1980s reached a scale that required the establishment of a separate facility. Research and development in this field was transferred to the new Packaging Innovation Center in Middletown, New York.

IP continued to consolidate other R & D activities at CRC. In 1986, Arizona Chemical's research and technical services group was transferred to CRC from Stamford, Connecticut, later followed by IP's white papers technical services group. When the Erling Riis Research Laboratory was closed in 1996, some of its functions were transferred to CRC, which expanded its office and laboratory space. The new space also accommodated the pulping research staff and CRC analytical services group.

DALHOUSIE, NEW BRUNSWICK PULP AND PAPER MILL

The construction of the Dalhousie mill in 1928 was part of International Paper president Archibald Graustein's strategic plan to improve the company's newsprint operations by expanding into Canada. Together with the Three Rivers and Gatineau mills in Quebec, Dalhousie formed the core of Canadian International Paper's newsprint division.

Dalhousie was sold in 1981 when IP divested itself of its Canadian holdings.

Dalhousie mill

DECORATIVE PRODUCTS

Covering a broad variety of items made by International Paper specialty businesses, decorative products include pressure laminates, particleboard, fiberboard, balancing veneers and graphic arts panels.

The foundations of what later became International Paper's decorative products operations were laid in 1969 with the formation of Uniwood. A production plant in Statesville, North Carolina, converted kraft paper into synthetic veneer backer sheets. In 1993, IP's Uniwood Division added a Fome-Cor® plant in Glasgow, Kentucky, producing polystyrene graphic arts products used for signs, point-of-purchase displays, photo printing and photo mounting. A year later, Uniwood became a central part of IP's new Decorative Products Division.

The National Plastics Company, formed in 1939 and later renamed Nevamar Corporation, was another prominent firm that became part of IP's decorative products operations. Originally producing high-pressure plastic laminates and synthetic fibers at its plant in Odenton, Maryland, the company later developed dimensional finishes for lami-

nates and the patented Armored Protection surface. Known for its Fountainhead® line, Nevamar produces a wide variety of decorative surface patterns used for countertops, furniture, flooring for computer rooms and related applications. Nevamar was acquired by IP in 1990.

In addition to Uniwood and Nevamar, the division included Micarta Industrial Laminates, formed in 1905 by George Westinghouse. Operating a manufacturing plant in Hampton, South Carolina, Micarta initially produced plastics used in resins, paper, cotton, fabrics and other products. Technology to produce postforming laminates for curved aircraft parts developed in World War II was later used to manufacture countertops with curved edges. In the 1950s, Micarta supplied glass melamine laminate for rocket noses and heat shields for Titan intercontinental ballistic missiles. A decade later, it developed copper-clad laminates for circuit boards for computers, television sets and cameras. Micarta was acquired by International Paper in 1995.

DISTRIBUTION

Prior to the 19th century, most paper mills operated in close proximity to urban centers where they sold their output directly to printers, newspapers and general merchants. This changed in the 1820s and 1830s, as an increasingly literate population demanded more newspapers, books, writing paper and envelopes, exceeding the capacity of local mills.

These market changes led to the establishment of wholesale merchant houses that bought paper products from the mills and marketed them to retailers, first in larger Northeastern cities and also later in other parts of the country. Some paper merchants operated as mill agents and brokers, obtaining orders for specialty paper and making arrangements for its production at the mill.

These specialty firms included Bulkley, Dunton & Company, a New York company founded in 1833 that later merged with other organizations and was acquired by International Paper. Western Newspaper Union, another distributor later acquired by IP, was founded in 1865 in Omaha, Nebraska, and traded in newsprint, printing equipment and supplies.

The late 19th century brought major changes to the pulp and paper industry that affected the distribution business. The introduction of groundwood pulp in the American paper industry in 1867 required extensive trading networks linking Northeastern manufacturers and newspapers all across the Eastern seaboard and the Midwest. Companies founded during the "groundwood pulp revolution" included Carter, Rice & Company, established in 1871, which first specialized in the New England newsprint trade and subsequently branched out into cardboard, book paper, stationery and related products. Paper merchants also marketed other new paper products developed during this era, including folding cartons, bags and corrugated packaging material.

Many firms that started in niche markets later added new product offerings and expanded the scope of their operations. Established in 1894 as a paper supply distributor in Minneapolis, Minnesota, the Leslie Paper Company later branched out into printing paper, school supplies, stationery, sanitary napkins and industrial paper. The Dixon Paper Company, founded in 1911 in Denver, Colorado, initially sold fine papers to local customers. Over the next several decades, it added industrial grades as well as graphic arts papers, equipment and supplies, and opened 14 warehouses in the Rocky Mountain states.

Some of the nation's leading paper distributors were acquired by the

Hammermill Paper Company from the 1960s to the 1980s. In 1961, it purchased the Western Newspaper Union, with 19 wholesale outlets in the Midwest. Establishing a pattern that continued during subsequent years, Hammermill allowed its new subsidiary to market products made by a variety of manufacturers instead of turning it into a "captive merchant."

Hammermill later acquired Carter Rice Storrs & Bement of Boston (a prestigious East Coast distributor), Commercial Distribution Associates (a group of paper merchant houses with branches in New England, the Mid-Atlantic states and Ohio), and Industrial Materials Distributors (a Cincinnati-based group operating in Ohio, Rhode Island, North Carolina and Ontario).

This extensive distribution network was expanded after Hammermill was acquired by

International Paper in 1986. Major additions included Dillard, Dixon, Leslie and Ingram Paper. In 1993, IP consolidated its $3 billion distribution business and renamed it ResourceNet International. IP did not turn ResourceNet International into a captive business; rather, the company focused on the customer and encouraged the distribution business to offer the customer the best products from around the world. The subsidiary was enabled to market products made by a wide range of suppliers. Operating in 250 locations at the time, ResourceNet International sold graphic arts supplies and equipment, printing paper, industrial packaging, janitorial and maintenance supplies, retail packaging and related products. In 1998, ResourceNet International was renamed xpedx.

ENVIRONMENTAL PROTECTION

International Paper's recognition of its environmental responsibilities dates to its earliest years. Hugh Chisholm decreed in 1901 that no immature trees would be harvested. Executives who followed also concentrated on forest-based programs, including the second president, who established the company's first tree nursery.

The company's regard for its forest resources included not only the planting and harvesting of trees for the manufacture of products but included the forest environment as well. In the 1950s, the company established guidelines providing protection for streams and wildlife habitats. These guidelines, then known as company Policy 11, codified management practices generally in use throughout the company at the time. As forest management practices evolved, the company remained in the forefront by pioneering new techniques that encompassed the entire forest resource: trees, land, water,

air, wildlife and human use. In 1994, the company and other members of the American Forest & Paper Association (AF&PA) joined to frame the Sustainable Forestry Initiative (SFI). The principles of SFI reflect the company's 1992 Forest Environmental Quality Guidelines and Forest Management Principles.

In 1943, International Paper joined with several other U.S. paper companies to form the National Council of the Paper Industry for Stream Improvement (NCSI). NCSI conducted research that led to stream improvements and wastewater treatment

technologies. Over the years the NCSI charter has been expanded to include research in all areas of the environment including forests. Today the organization is called the National Council for Air and Stream Improvement (NCASI).

Also during the 1940s the company began to fund environmental research at universities. One of the early studies involved the effects on cows that were drinking water from streams containing effluent from the company's paper mills in Bastrop, Louisiana. No adverse effects were found.

One of the earliest projects to reduce the impact of wastewater on receiving streams was the construction of Wham Brake near Bastrop, Louisiana. Wham Brake was an impoundment basin that held treated wastewater from the Bastrop and Louisiana mills, allowing the water to be discharged during high river flows to minimize impact.

At the Moss Point mill in the 1960s, the company pioneered the processes for dewatering sludge and burning the sludge in incinerators to reduce landfill disposal.

During the 1960s the company's environmental remediation efforts paralleled the actions of the government's new Environmental Protection Agency (EPA), as well as similar agencies created at state and local government levels. At that time, EPA concentrated on building regulatory frameworks for compliance with the Clean Air and Clean Water Acts.

Before the deadlines for complying with the original Clean Water Act went into effect, mills throughout International Paper

either had installed or were installing secondary wastewater treatment systems. These systems significantly reduced the impact on streams and rivers into which they discharged. Many of these secondary systems were just that, secondary, being added to the process behind primary wastewater clarifiers previously installed in the late 1950s and early 1960s.

In air pollution abatement, the company moved quickly to reduce a prime regulatory concern of particulate emissions, installing electrostatic precipitators on its boilers, which removed more than 95 percent of particulates. International Paper also complied with the new Superfund legislation, an EPA administered program which identified sites requiring environmental remediation.

The detection of minute particles of dioxin in the streams below several U. S. paper mills in 1985 had a tremendous impact on the industry. Unsure that dioxin was attributable to paper mills, International Paper and other forest products companies joined with EPA to determine the source. The study revealed that dioxin was a by-product of the pulp bleaching process. Though no conclusive evidence linked dioxin to a number of alleged health risks, International Paper moved quickly to eliminate dioxin from its mill effluents.

The company virtually eliminated dioxin, at a cost of more than $150 million, by implementing new technological processes that were elemental chlorine free. Pioneered at the Moss Point mill in the early 1990s, the company had, by the end of 1996, implemented this bleaching process in all but two of its mills worldwide with the final two mills, formerly part of Federal Paper Board, scheduled for conversion by the end of 1998.

In 1989, IP became a participant in a new program called the Industrial Toxics Project (ITP). Initiated by EPA, ITP was a voluntary chemical release reduction initiative. Its goal was a 50 percent reduction in specific chemicals by year's end 1995. International Paper surpassed EPA's goal by achieving an 82.5 percent reduction.

Today, the company remains true to its environmental heritage – a heritage initiated with the forest and expanded into an overall commitment for environmental best practices at every company location.

ERIE RESEARCH CENTER

The Erie Research Center, built by the Hammermill Paper Company in a period of rapid corporate expansion during the 1960s, was designed to develop new products and processes supporting the company's growth. Originally named the Corporate Technical Center, it opened in 1966 and housed the corporate technical group and the engineering group. The center was located near the corporate headquarters and the paper mill in Erie, Pennsylvania, enabling the two research and development groups to keep close relationships with the practical side of the paper business.

During the first several years, the center's work on pulping focused on the optimization of the Neutracel® process, a modified neutral semi-chemical process using Northern hardwoods. Because there was no black liquor recovery process, the effluent problem was severe. As a result, the center also developed an alternate pulping procedure that permitted chemical recovery. This led to the development of Neutracel® II, a modified soda process suitable for recovery that provided Hammermill's Erie mill with excellent, low-cost pulp for fine papers. Neutracel II also enabled the company to meet environmental regulations for air and water pollution control.

Product development meanwhile focused on grades for the Xerox Corporation and the development of No. 4 bond grades. Hammermill was a major Xerox supplier and followed its development of photocopiers with papers tailor-made for Xerox machines. This was accomplished through a product development committee that included marketing, research and manufacturing representatives. Other product development projects involved fine papers for Hammermill and its subsidiaries, the Beckett Paper Company and the Strathmore Paper Company, and industrial papers for other Hammermill subsidiaries.

The use of alkaline sizing technology for grades produced by Hammermill emerged as a major area of development during the late 1970s. The potential for improved product quality and cost savings was recognized, but the practical problems of implementing this technology required significant research. Once these problems had been solved, alkaline sizing technology was introduced in Hammermill and IP mills.

In 1989, three years after Hammermill had merged with IP, the center was renamed the Erie Research Center.

ERLING RIIS RESEARCH LABORATORY

Until 1946, International Paper's Southern mill system did not operate a formal research and development organization. Its R & D projects were managed and staffed by mill employees, who conducted laboratory work and scale-up activities in each mill. In 1946, the Mobile Research Laboratory was established in the basement of the Mobile, Alabama, mill to perform R & D for the Southern Kraft Division. The laboratory moved to its own building in 1952, which was renamed in 1961 to honor Erling Riis. A former vice president and general manager of the Southern Kraft Division, Riis was a strong proponent of technical innovation and had been instrumental in establishing the facility.

The laboratory's first major research initiatives during the late 1940s included an effort to improve continuous digester technology. IP researchers developed a technique to reduce damage to fibers during the discharge of the digester. In close cooperation with Canadian International Paper's pulp mill and research laboratory in Hawkesbury, Ontario, the Mobile laboratory also developed a method to use the kraft process to make dissolving pulp from hardwoods. Initiated by Erling Riis and John Gilbert, a senior research scientist, this innovation enabled IP to use Southern hardwoods, which had rarely been used to make pulp and paper. The commercial result of this work was the Natchez, Mississippi, pulp mill, which began operating in 1950.

Building on their accomplishments in hardwood research, the laboratory's scientists and technicians developed a production process for lightweight white papers made from 100 percent hardwood pulp. This allowed the conversion of the Mobile mill's No. 2 machine from kraft grades to lightweight bleached papers in 1957.

In the early 1960s, what was now known as the Erling Riis Research Laboratory (ERRL) led a multimillion dollar research program to develop the foil-laminated Pure-Pak carton. This packaging innovation featured superior barrier qualities and was used as a syrup container by soft drink producers. The laboratory staff supported the commercialization of the carton at the Pine Bluff mill in Arkansas. In a separate initiative launched during this period, ERRL participated in the development of computer-controlled paper machines at IP's Georgetown, South Carolina, mill and other facilities.

ERRL reached another milestone in the late 1960s with the development of Acetakraft®, an acetate dissolving pulp used in the manufacture of textiles and cigarette filters. The research was commercialized at the Natchez mill in 1968.

The 1970s witnessed new research on process technology, such as displacement bleaching and oxygen delignification. ERRL's contributions to product development included the Pure-Pak oil carton and the first board suitable for microwave ovens.

In the 1980s, as International Paper embarked upon a capital expenditure development and expansion program, ERRL tested new production methods and technologies that were later applied at several IP mills, including new forming processes, chip quality optimization systems and the computerized monitoring of wet-end analysis.

With the opening of IP's Packaging Development Center (PDC) near Cincinnati, Ohio in 1996, the major portion of the work done at ERRL was transferred to the PDC, the Corporate Research Center in Sterling Forest, New York, and the Erie Research Center. In 1997, the last group was transferred from Mobile to Cincinnati and ERRL was closed.

FEDERAL PAPER BOARD COMPANY

Organized in 1916, the Federal Paper Board Company became part of IP in 1996 in one of the largest mergers in the American pulp and paper industry.

William Shortess

William Shortess founded Federal Paper Board when he purchased a medium-sized recycled paperboard mill in Bogota, New Jersey. The new company soon acquired eight additional mills, including a large facility in Versailles, Connecticut, and modernized their equipment and facilities. Specializing in recycled paperboard made from wastepaper, the company supplied board converters that manufactured folding cartons for consumer products.

The fledgling operation suffered financial setbacks in the volatile paperboard market, forcing creditors to take control in 1929. The Great Depression of the 1930s wreaked further havoc. A turning point was reached in 1943, however, after three employees—Howard Brown, Guy Freas, and John R. Kennedy, Sr.—acquired the company from the founder's estate and named Kennedy chief executive officer, a position he occupied until 1975.

During his tenure, Kennedy and his team transformed Federal from a $7 million paperboard company into a $200 million enterprise with diverse business interests in the pulp, paper, converting and wood products sectors. In the late 1940s, the company entered the paperboard converting business after it built carton plants in Versailles, Connecticut, and Bogota, New Jersey.

Acquisitions, beginning with the purchase in 1953 of National Folding Box Company, which operated a board mill and carton plant in New Haven, Connecticut, strengthened Federal's position as a paperboard converter. To raise money for this ambitious expansion program, Kennedy and his associates took the Federal Paper Board Company public in 1953 with an initial offering of 200,000 shares. Two years later, the Federal Paper Board Company was listed on the New York Stock Exchange.

In the 1960s, Federal began consolidating its paperboard carton converting operations. It closed down several facilities, including the original mill in Bogota, New Jersey, and obsolete plants in Montville, Connecticut, and Belleville, New Jersey. The company also built the Sprague mill, a recycled paperboard mill in Versailles, Connecticut, the largest in the world at the time and the last of its kind built in the United States. During its early years of operation, the Sprague mill produced recycled linerboard, but slack demand resulted in considerable financial losses. Conditions improved in 1968 when the mill switched to recycled paperboard and began supplying Nabisco Brands' folding carton division, its main customer during subsequent years.

In 1972, the Federal Paper Board Company acquired a solid bleached sulfate paperboard and market pulp mill in Riegelwood, North Carolina, along with 350,000 acres of timberland. A sawmill erected the following year in Armour, North Carolina, supplied the Riegelwood mill with wood chips. It also produced lumber for the building industry, marking the beginning of Federal's wood products business. The growth of this business led to the construction of a second sawmill in Newberry, South Carolina.

In 1975, John R. Kennedy, Sr., who had overseen Federal Paper Board's extraordinary expansion and growth during the postwar decades, retired. He was succeeded by his son, John R. Kennedy, Jr. In 1985, the younger Kennedy accomplished a major feat by engineering a $317 million purchase of key assets of the Continental Group. These assets included a paperboard mill and a saw mill in Augusta, Georgia, and saw mills in Washington, Georgia, and Johnston, South Carolina. With the acquisitions, Federal became the nation's second-largest bleached paperboard company. Extensive upgrading of the Augusta paperboard plant made it the world's largest coated solid bleached sulfate paperboard mill.

Like International Paper, Federal launched an international expansion program in the late 1980s that added sales offices in Britain, Japan and Switzerland. Solidifying its foothold in international markets, the company acquired Thomas Tait & Sons, Ltd., a Scottish producer of uncoated paper whose Inverurie mill became Federal's first overseas manufacturing facility.

At home, the company reconfigured its converting operations, shifting the emphasis from folding cartons to paper cups. It sold some of its folding carton plants, leaving only the North Carolina facilities in Durham, Hendersonville, and Wilmington, and a plant in Thomaston, Georgia. In 1989, it acquired Imperial Cup Corporation, with plants in Kenton, Ohio; LaFayette, Georgia; Salisbury, Maryland; and Visalia, California. A year later, it acquired Continental Bondware, Incorporated, and merged the two subsidiaries to form Imperial Bondware, one of the largest manufacturers in the paper cup industry. To integrate the cup business more fully into its overall operations, Federal built a poly-extrusion facility in Prosperity, South Carolina, which processed the paperboard produced at the Riegelwood and Augusta mills and supplied the company's new cup plants and the folding carton industry.

With its core business in paperboard production and conversion, as well as a major presence in the market pulp and wood products sector, Federal was a suitable candidate for a merger with International Paper. The two companies completed successful negotiations in 1996, completing the $3.5 billion merger.

FOLDING CARTONS

Folding cartons—the leading packaging product used for cereal, dryfoods, cosmetics and hundreds of other items—fold at the creases and can be shipped flat from the carton plant to the packaging facility.

The first folding carton was produced in 1879, when a printer used the sharp edges of his printing plates to cut bag-grade paper into a box shape, and the dull edges to make crease lines so the paper could fold without ripping. The introduction of folding cartons during the late 19th century enabled manufacturers of mass-produced consumer items to package their goods individually and economically for the first time. Folding carton manufacturers devised new printing techniques which allowed consumer goods producers to decorate boxes with logos and images. More visually attractive paperboard grades, such as bleached kraft, also became available during the 1930s for use in folding cartons.

In 1939, International Paper's mill at Springhill, Louisiana, became the first in the company to produce bleached kraft grades for folding cartons on the Fourdrinier machine. IP entered the folding carton business directly in 1958 with its acquisition of Lord Baltimore Press, a leading producer of multiple-color boxes. As IP's folding carton business expanded, the company built or acquired plants in Camarillo, California; Clinton, Iowa; Cincinnati, Ohio; Hendersonville, North Carolina; Hopkinsville, Kentucky; Thomaston, Georgia; Richmond, Virginia; and Wilmington, North Carolina.

Throughout its history, IP's folding carton division has provided extensive technical services to customers. In 1996, the division expanded these services and consolidated them at the Packaging Development Center in Cincinnati, Ohio. The center's services include materials research, product development, packaging-systems design and engineering, and customized printing.

Facility Location	Year built/ acquired
Mobile, Alabama	1930
Clinton, Iowa	1958
Cincinnati (Springdale), Ohio	1962
Wilmington, North Carolina	1974
Jackson, Tennessee *	1978
Richmond, Virginia *	1980
Hopkinsville, Kentucky	1982
Bowling Green, Kentucky	1993
Hendersonville, North Carolina *	1996
LaGrange, Georgia *	1996
Loveland, Ohio	1996
Thomaston, Georgia *	1996

*acquired

FORT EDWARD, NEW YORK PULP AND PAPER MILL

Located in upstate New York, the Fort Edward mill was acquired by International Paper shortly after the company's formation in 1898. The mill operated seven newsprint machines. After stiff competition from inexpensive Canadian producers forced IP to phase out newsprint production at this and other Northeastern mills during the mid-1920s, Fort Edward switched to making book and bond grades.

The Fort Edward mill was sold to the Scott Paper Company in 1944.

Fort Edward mill

FOURDRINIER PAPER MACHINE

A Fourdrinier paper machine, which can be longer than a football field, produces a continuous sheet of paper. A solution of about one percent fiber and 99 percent water flows onto a moving endless screen that drains enough of the water to form a sheet of intermingled fibers. The sheet then passes through a series of presses that mechanically remove additional water and then through a series of steam-heated dryer cans before being wound onto a reel.

The continuous paper-forming machine was invented in France in 1799 by Nicholas-Louis Robert but developed in England with the financial support of Henry and Sealy Fourdrinier, London stationers. Although named for the brothers, the first practical paper machine was designed by the Englishman Bryan Donkin and began operating in 1804.

GARDINER, OREGON PULP AND PAPER MILL

In March 1964, IP started up its first pulp and paper mill on the West Coast at Gardiner, Oregon. The one-machine facility, which cost $35 million to build, produced 100,000 tons of unbleached kraft linerboard and kraft paper per year. Gardiner supplied IP's West Coast corrugated container plants, and customers in Oregon, Washington and California.

Gardiner received most of its wood chip supplies from a wood products plant at Reedsport, Oregon, operated by IP's Long-Bell Division. The John H. Hinman Tree Farm, a 400,000-acre forestland located near the mill, also served as a source of raw materials.

Extensive renovations were made at the mill during the 1970s and 1980s, including the installation of a new recovery boiler, a 14-unit dryer section, new primary and secondary head boxes and gloss calender rolls. In addition to Pineliner® high-performance and Hydrokraft® wet-strength grades, Gardiner produces KlaWhite® linerboard and supplies domestic and Far Eastern markets.

GATINEAU, QUEBEC PULP AND PAPER MILL

The newsprint mill in Gatineau, Quebec, began operations with four machines and a daily production of 400 tons. Located on the Ottawa River near 6,000 square miles of timberlands controlled by Canadian International Paper (CIP), Gatineau became a center of Canadian newsprint production.

Gatineau was sold in 1981 when IP divested itself of its Canadian holdings.

GEORGETOWN, SOUTH CAROLINA PULP AND PAPER MILL

Completed in less than nine months, International Paper's Georgetown kraft mill became fully operational in August 1937. Initially a two-machine mill, it received a third Fourdrinier in 1941, making Georgetown the world's largest paper mill at the time.

During World War II, the mill's No. 3 machine produced wet-strength linerboard for use in military packaging. In 1942, a separate container plant was built to convert linerboard into corrugated boxes. Soon after the war, Georgetown converted its No. 1 machine to Chem Fibre®, an innovative board grade developed by IP that was made from 100 percent hardwood pulp.

In 1961, a six-stage bleach plant was installed at Georgetown, enabling its No. 2 machine to produce tabulating index paper for IBM computers. The following year, building upon its evolving relationship with IBM, Georgetown became one of the first American paper mills to experiment with computerized information and process control systems. IP technicians worked with data-processing engineers from IBM and with consultants from Arthur Andersen to develop and refine the system. The Georgetown trials demonstrated the system's value for improving process and financial controls, and it subsequently was adapted by other IP locations.

The 1980s brought changes to better serve the customers of the Georgetown mill. Centralization of the finishing and shipping area was completed, and a major reconfiguration of the mill began in 1982. In 1983, the first stage of the mill transformation occurred with the start-up of the A-line bleach plant. The A-line handled 100 percent pine pulp, and later, in the same year, its counterpart B-line was put into operation to handle 100 percent hardwood pulp.

In 1984, a new woodyard was built to handle full tree-length round wood (both pine and hardwood). Also, a new recaustisizing chemical preparation area was constructed. The pulp mill/bleach plant reconfiguration included the C-line, the largest continuous digester and displacement bleach plant in the world for pine pulp production. Batch digesters were upgraded for hardwood production. In the fall of 1984, the No. 3 pulp machine started producing pine market pulp and Supersoft®.

Just over one year from the announcement of the mill's major reconfiguration, Phase 1 of construction was completed. The No. 1 machine was totally rebuilt. For the first time, the mill was producing lightweight white paper, including offset, tablet, envelope and forms bond, with a capacity of 600,000 tons per year.

Georgetown mill

GLENS FALLS, NEW YORK PULP AND PAPER MILL

Located in upstate New York, the Glens Falls Paper Company joined 16 paper companies to form International Paper in 1898. During the early 1890s, the Glens Falls mill formed a Canadian subsidiary named the St. Maurice Lumber Company that later became part of Canadian International Paper.

When newsprint production declined in the Northeastern states, Glens Falls experimented with a variety of new products. This included a tissue product used in surgical dressings and as a sanitary absorbent, first produced in 1926. In 1941, IP sold the mill to the Scott Paper Company, a major tissue producer.

GLENS FALLS RESEARCH LABORATORY

Organized in 1901 as IP's Central Test Bureau, the Glens Falls laboratory in upstate New York was the first of its kind in the American pulp and paper industry. Its initial function was to improve and standardize production methods in the company's Northeastern mills. At each mill, foremen took pulp and paper samples and shipped them to Glens Falls, where a scientist conducted a series of tests to determine composition, thickness and strength. The bureau also developed new standards for sulfite, bleaching compounds and numerous other components that were used in the papermaking process.

To run pilot projects, the laboratory's superintendent, Dr. Rudolf De Roode, imported a scale-model paper machine from Germany, where papermakers had pioneered the use of miniature Fourdriniers. At Glens Falls, scientists and craftsmen used this fully operational machine in experiments with new types of pulp to determine their potential for commercial production.

Renamed the Glens Falls Research Laboratory in 1930, the facility served as a research and development center for mills in IP's Northern Division. It provided technical support for Northeastern mills as they converted from newsprint to book grades. During the Great Depression of the 1930s, Glens Falls was forced to reduce its research staff. The remaining staff directed its efforts away from long-range research and concentrated solely on applied research and operating problems in the mills. After World War II, the staff increased to 50 people, most of whom participated in long-range research programs.

During the 1960s, the aging laboratory became overcrowded and closed in 1969. Most staff members and programs were moved to IP's new Corporate Research Center at Sterling Forest, New York.

HAMILTON, OHIO PAPER MILL

The Hamilton, Ohio, mill began operations in 1848, producing 2,000 pounds of newsprint daily from rag pulp. After two years, the mill added another machine to supply its largest customer, *The Cincinnati Gazette*. In 1887, the company was incorporated as the Beckett Paper Company. Thomas Beckett developed a high-quality, color cover paper in 1894, "Buckeye Cover," which became one of the company's long-lasting and recognizable brands. In 1905, the original mill was razed and replaced with a new plant.

Hammermill Paper Company purchased the Beckett Paper Company in 1959, adding 35,000 tons of paper to Hammermill's annual production capacity. The Hamilton mill became part of International Paper when the latter acquired Hammermill in 1986. Hamilton is the company's oldest continuously operating mill in the United States. Changes underway at this time make the facility competitive in the printing paper business as it prepares for its 150th anniversary celebration in 1998.

HAMMERMILL PAPER COMPANY

Long recognized as a world leader in fine papers, the Hammermill Paper Company was acquired by IP in 1986.

Hammermill was founded in Erie, Pennsylvania, in 1898 by Moritz Behrend and his sons Ernst and Otto. The Behrends were native Germans who had run a successful papermaking company in Hammermühle, Germany for decades. Their Erie mill, featuring a sulfite pulp digester and two paper machines, specialized in sulfite bond paper. Based on the newly developed sulfite pulping process, this high-quality grade replaced rag-content writing papers. Although customers initially resisted the company's new product, Hammermill soon established itself as a leader in the fine papers market.

In 1912, Hammermill doubled its production capacity by adding two additional paper machines. That same year, the company introduced Hammermill Bond, its first mill-watermarked product. Prior to this strategic move, Hammermill had produced fine papers that bore the individual watermarks of paper merchants. The decision to replace these private lines with a mill-watermarked grade reflected Hammermill's legendary marketing abilities. Indeed, the company's own national advertising campaign pitched Hammermill as "the best known name in paper." Hammermill Bond and its companion products were sold through select paper merchants and the company's own sales people, who focused their efforts on developing strong relationships with customers.

Duplicating the German system of generous employee benefits, Hammermill's president Moritz Behrend introduced paid vacations in 1919, when such a policy was unheard of in the American pulp and paper industry. Long before other employers adopted similar policies, Hammermill also instituted an employee profit-sharing plan and supported workers' social and athletic activities. Close ties between workers and management remained a hallmark of industrial relations even during the Depression, when Hammermill avoided lay-offs and introduced the eight-hour day in 1933. Once the Depression bottomed out in the late 1930s, the Erie mill increased its production capacity by adding the No. 6 paper machine.

Hammermill's president, Ernst Behrend, died in 1940 and was succeeded by Norman Wilson. Under his leadership, Hammermill contributed to industrial mobilization during World War II. In addition to supplying the U. S. Army and the Government Printing Office with writing papers, the company produced a range of military items, including plastic rocket launchers and plywood assault boats. The war also marked the beginning of organized collective bargaining when the United Mine Workers Union was certified as the bargaining agent for Hammermill employees in 1943.

The postwar years brought a surge in demand for bond paper that led to the installation of the No. 7 paper machine in 1947. The boom was interrupted the following year by a materials shortage created when Ontario, Hammermill's main source of pulpwood, announced cutbacks in softwood exports. The latter triggered an intensive search for a substitute, which resulted in the development of Neutracel®, a low-cost, high-quality pulp made from hardwoods that grew close to the Erie mill in northwestern Pennsylvania. To raise money for the commercial production of Neutracel, Hammermill went public and was listed on the New York Stock Exchange in 1952. Neutracel quickly became the company's most successful pulp product.

Hammermill scored a marketing success when it developed and became the sole authorized manufacturer of paper used in photocopiers produced by the Xerox Corporation. Demand skyrocketed during the 1950s, when many offices acquired their first Xerox machines.

Hammermill began a major expansion program in the late 1950s that continued over the next two decades. To provide an outlet for its extensive pulp production capacities at the Erie mill, Hammermill acquired the Beckett Paper Company of Hamilton, Ohio, in 1959. Two years later, it purchased a specialty mill in Oswego, New York, and the Strathmore Paper Company, a leading manufacturer of cotton-based paper with mills in Woronoco and Mittineague, Massachusetts.

In 1961, Hammermill strengthened its distribution business by acquiring the Western Newspaper Union, a wholesale operation with 19 outlets that marketed paper, printing supplies and printing equipment. Several years later, Hammermill also acquired the Boston-based Carter Rice Storrs & Bement Company, a respected paper distributor operating branches on the East Coast.

With five paper mills and only one major pulp production facility in Erie, Hammermill decided to expand its pulping capacities. In 1965, it built the Riverdale pulp mill near Selma, Alabama. On the pulp converting side, the company acquired a coated-book paper mill at Lock Haven, Pennsylvania in 1965 that expanded Hammermill's product line. Four years later, the Hammermill family of companies was joined by the Thilmany Paper Company of Kaukauna, Wisconsin, a well-known producer of specialty kraft grades.

Expansion into new markets during the 1960s helped the company weather the difficult 1970s. Inflation, strikes and fierce competition wreaked havoc in the fine paper sector, but the strong performance of Thilmany and the distribution business limited losses. Further strengthening Thilmany's position in industrial papers, Hammermill acquired Akrosil, a Wisconsin-based producer of silicone-coated papers and films. In a related move, Hammermill in 1985 acquired the Nicolet Paper Company of DePere, Wisconsin, a leading producer of backing papers for pressure-sensitive labels and tapes.

Hammermill also established sawmill operations in Alabama by building plants in Maplesville and Tuscaloosa in 1975 and 1982. To enhance wood products marketing, Hammermill acquired the McEwen Lumber Company, a Southeastern lumber distributor, in 1982.

Meanwhile, the company improved the financial performance of its core operations by producing a broader range of mill-brand papers at its existing plants. In the 1980s, it acquired the Millers Falls Paper Company of Massachusetts, a specialist in premium papers, and installed the No. 15 paper machine at its Riverdale mill.

In this era, when hostile takeovers ravaged American business, Hammermill confronted two attempts by corporate raiders to take control of the company. The first, launched in 1980 by Carl Icahn, who demanded the sale of many valuable acquisitions and distribution of the proceeds in the form of dividends, was defeated by the company's stockholders. The second was initiated by corporate raider Paul Bilzerian. Stepping in, IP acquired Hammermill for $1.1 billion in 1986.

The transaction benefited both parties. IP gained an important foothold in the high-quality paper market, learned valuable lessons from Hammermill's marketing experts who were considered the best in the paper business, and took control of a distribution business that was later reorganized as ResourceNet International (later renamed xpedx). Building on IP's strengths, Hammermill streamlined its manufacturing operations and improved profitability.

Several former Hammermill properties received extensive renovations during the 1990s. The Riverdale mill, for example, completed a $350 million improvement program that included the No. 16 paper machine, one of the nation's largest de-inking facilities, other recycling equipment and a new gas turbine generator.

HAWKESBURY, ONTARIO PULP MILL, RESEARCH LABORATORY

The Hawkesbury pulp mill in Ontario, Canada, was built in 1898 by the Riordon Paper Company, Ltd. It was designed by Richard Cullen, a prominent papermaker, who later served as president and chairman of International Paper. During the early years, Hawkesbury, one of Canada's first sulfite pulp mills, produced book-grade pulp. Originally equipped for an annual output capacity of 23,000 tons, it increased its pulp volume to 60,000 tons in 1918. Five years later, Hawkesbury built a laboratory that specialized in wood cellulose research.

Shortly after IP acquired Hawkesbury and other Riordon operations in 1925, the mill was incorporated into Canadian International Paper (CIP). The laboratory served as CIP's central research and development facility. Its accomplishments included the development of chlorine dioxide for bleaching pulp and hardwood dissolving pulp. The Hawkesbury laboratory also helped develop prehydrolized kraft hardwood dissolving pulp that enabled IP to use Southern hardwoods; in this venture, it worked closely with IP's research laboratory in Mobile, Alabama, and the Natchez, Mississippi, mill where the process was commercialized.

The Hawkesbury pulp mill switched from book-grade to dissolving pulp and became North America's leading rayon pulp supplier. It was sold in 1981, when IP divested itself of its Canadian holdings.

HUDSON RIVER PULP AND PAPER MILL, CORINTH, NEW YORK

Hudson River is the only one of International Paper's original 17 mills still owned and operated by the company.

Built in 1869 by Albrecht Pagenstecher and other pioneers of the American pulp and paper industry, the mill was among the nation's first producers of wood-based pulp. Its first two paper machines began operating in 1872 and produced fine printing paper. Located at Corinth, New York on the Hudson River, which supplied power and water for the papermaking process, the mill complex included a dam which was rebuilt several times. During the 1880s, it installed what was then the largest paper making machine in North America with a 112-inch wire running at 250 feet per minute.

When Hudson River joined IP in 1898, it was widely considered the company's flagship mill. It operated nine paper machines, all of which were soon converted to newsprint. Another machine was installed in 1914 to produce coarse wrapping paper.

During the 1920s, the mill developed innovative waste disposal technologies that turned sulfite liquor into a material used in road construction and foundries. Upon completion of a reconfiguration, Hudson River switched from newsprint to printing grades in 1941. To enhance its ability to compete in this high-value product line, the mill added blade coaters to its paper machines during the 1950s and 1960s to produce coated grades.

The shutdown of the No. 10 machine in 1980 left Hudson River with three machines that produced coated groundwood and free sheet publication papers. In 1993, the mill added a de-inking system that enabled it to produce high-quality offset paper consisting of 10 percent de-inked fibers and up to 50 percent total recycled fibers. The system enabled the mill to turn old books and office waste paper into coated printing paper sold under the names of Adirondack®, Saratoga® and Miraweb II®.

Hudson River mill

IMAGING PRODUCTS

Prior to the 1990s, imaging products were defined as photographic film, paper and process chemicals. Today, they also include digital products and reproduction systems.

International Paper entered the imaging products market in the late 1980s with the acquisitions of Anitec, a manufacturer of graphic arts products based in Binghamton, New York, and Cookson Graphics and Horsell with plants in Leeds, Britain and Munich, Germany. These companies specialized in photographic films, papers and plates for the printing market. In 1989, IP also acquired Ilford, Britain's largest commercial film products company with manufacturing facilities at Mobberley, England, and Fribourg, Switzerland. Building on a tradition that reached back to its formation in 1880, Ilford pioneered monochrome imaging products and later added color films and paper for professional photographers.

In 1991, IP's imaging subsidiaries introduced 16 new color films and other innovative products. Demand for photosensitive film and paper declined during the early 1990s when digital imaging products started to dominate the market.

International Paper offered the division for sale in 1997.

IMPERIAL BONDWARE CORPORATION

A major producer of foodservice packaging products such as cups, lids, cartons, trays, containers and plates, Imperial Bondware was formed in 1990, combining Continental Bondware and the Imperial Cup Company.

Continental Bondware traced its roots to 1946, when the Continental Container Company established a paper container division through the acquisition of the Boothby Container Company of the Mono Service Company of Newark, New Jersey. Capitalizing on the growing use of disposable foodservice items after World War II, the division produced disposable cups and later also paper plates. During the 1950s, it acquired the Bowes Industry Company of Three Rivers, Michigan, and the American Paper Goods Company of Kensington, Connecticut. Continental's paper container division was renamed Continental Bondware in 1957.

Continental Bondware performed well until the 1970s, when styrofoam products started to capture a growing market share. Attempts to enter this product line through the acquisition of Crest Container, a styrofoam manufacturer, failed, resulting in financial losses during the late 1970s. This facilitated a reorganization in 1979 which included the closure of three plants and Crest Container. Focusing on its core business in paper cups and popcorn containers, Continental Bondware recovered during subsequent years and was acquired by the Kiewit-Murdoch Group, which launched a $40 million expansion program. In 1990, Continental Bondware was acquired by the Federal Paper Board Company, which combined its operations with those of the Imperial Cup Company to form Imperial Bondware.

Imperial Cup was formed in 1968 by the Allen family of Kenton, Ohio, to secure a steady supply of high-quality paper cups for its vending machine business. Developing a thriving business in selling cups to outside vending machine operators, Imperial Cup later opened three production plants. After acquiring the Holiday Cup Company of Wisconsin in 1985, Imperial Cup itself was acquired by the Federal Paper Board Company in 1989 and combined with Continental Bondware to form Imperial Bondware.

Originally operating six production facilities, Imperial Bondware consolidated into three plants and maintained manufacturing operations at Visalia, California; Shelbyville, Illinois; and Kenton, Ohio. It joined IP in 1996, when the Federal Paper Board Company merged with International Paper.

INDUSTRIAL RELATIONS

When International Paper was founded in 1898, shop floor operations were run by senior craftsmen who hired, fired and disciplined members of their crews. A strict hierarchy existed between ordinary workers and their crew "bosses," some of whom were organized in exclusive craft unions. To form a direct relationship with IP's management and curb the bosses' often arbitrary exercise of power, IP workers joined Laborers' Protective Unions that were affiliated with the American Federation of Labor (AFL). Although many IP managers initially disapproved of these organizations, they later realized that organized collective bargaining could benefit both the company and its workers. In 1902, IP signed the first labor contract in the American pulp and paper industry with the Laborers' Protective Union representing workers from Ticonderoga, New York; Livermore Falls, Maine; and other IP mills. The contract replaced informal agreements between bosses and crew members with a fixed system of wages and hours.

In 1906, the Laborers' Protective Union locals joined forces with other trade unions and founded the International Brotherhood of Pulp, Sulfite, and Paper Mill Workers (later to become part of the United Paperworkers International Union). Following several tough battles, IP and the International Brotherhood signed a milestone agreement in 1912, in which the company recognized the union as its official partner in the collective bargaining process. The contract was also signed by other trade unions representing electrical workers, steam fitters, plumbers, carpenters and machinists.

Management and organized labor remained on friendly terms for the next several years and concluded successful contract negotiations from 1914 to 1920. In the wake of World War I, however, IP found itself in dire financial straits because it could not compete with low-cost Canadian newsprint producers. It demanded that the union accept a wage reduction, but organized labor balked. This contributed to the "Great Paper War of 1921," when strikes and lockouts

raged in many IP communities. The company expelled the union and instituted an open shop policy.

Although collective bargaining ceased until the 1930s, International Paper and its employees developed an innovative system of industrial relations. IP's Quarter Century Society, established in 1923, promoted social activities between company officers and employees who had been connected with the company for 25 years or more. That same year also marked the beginning of the Employees' Mutual Benefit Association (EMBA) which provided members with life insurance, disability benefits and protection against non-occupational accidents. Moreover, IP published a monthly newsletter that kept employees up-to-date on local events and company affairs.

Collective bargaining resumed during the Great Depression of the 1930s, when IP developed a more favorable view of the International Brotherhood of Pulp, Sulfite, and Paper Mill Workers. This important change in the company's attitude toward organized labor was the work of a new generation of International Paper managers led by Richard Cullen. In 1937, one year after Cullen had been named president of IP, senior management and union leaders agreed on procedures to organize IP's workforce in the United States and Canada. This paved the way for a series of successful union elections and contract negotiations, particularly at IP's Southern Kraft Division, whose management actively encouraged employees to join the International Brotherhood of Pulp, Sulfite, and Paper Mill Workers. The Southern Kraft Division also developed a multiple mill group labor contract in which a single contract was negotiated for all its mills.

During the postwar era, negotiations between the Southern Kraft Division and the unions were usually held in Mobile, Alabama, and Jackson, Mississippi. Southern Kraft's labor contract was considered the most important in the industry because it served as a model for most other collective bargaining agreements. IP's Northern Division, which included plants in New York and New England, also negotiated multiple

mill group labor contracts, but several mills signed their own separate agreements with the unions. In many IP towns, union locals became an important part of community life and maintained good relations with mill managers.

In the segregated South, white and African American workers were organized in separate locals, which negotiated separate contracts with the company. Accepted practice of the time barred African American employees from rising through the ranks and gaining seniority rights. This changed in the early 1960s, when union locals were merged to eliminate racial identity, and all lines of progression were opened to all employees. In 1968, the company and unions negotiated the Jackson Memorandum, which provided a means for African Americans to reach their rightful place in the line of progression of their choice.

Strike activity remained low compared to earlier decades because most conflicts were resolved at the bargaining table. Exceptions included the only work stoppage in the history of the Southern Kraft Division (22

days in 1965) followed by a number of isolated and sporadic strikes in the mill system.

Organized labor played an important role in the modernization of IP's industrial base in the 1980s. After much internal argument, the unions agreed in 1984 to end the multiple mill group labor contract system. Beginning in 1983, locals across the country agreed to phase out extra pay for Sunday work, with the exception of locals at Jay, Maine; Lock Haven, Pennsylvania; and De Pere, Wisconsin, which struck in June 1987. Anticipating a strike at its Mobile, Alabama, mill, IP locked out mill employees in March 1987. These conflicts ended in the fall of 1988 when the unions unilaterally ended the strikes. A few weeks later, a new labor agreement was signed at the Mobile mill, ending the lockout. Industrial relations remained tense for several years after the 1987 conflict. In 1993, however, IP and the United Paperworkers International Union negotiated a "peace accord" in which they agreed to return to the positive relationship of earlier years.

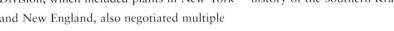

INTERNATIONAL PAPER COMPANY FOUNDATION

The International Paper Company Foundation was incorporated in 1953 to provide financial support to secondary education in more than a dozen school districts where IP maintained production facilities. Early grants focused on reading programs, improvements of school guidance services, student involvement in school government and related activities. The Foundation also sponsored annual conferences for administrators and teachers, offered summer scholarships for teachers at Columbia University's Teachers College, Auburn University, and Tuskegee Institute, and provided financial assistance for research

assistants contributing to its programs. During the early 1970s, a matching contribution plan matched IP employees' gifts to educational institutions up to an annual limit of $1,500 per employee. In addition to supporting educational programs, the Foundation provided financial assistance to health, social welfare and urban affairs groups.

The Foundation later expanded its focus, supporting education in kindergarten and elementary schools. In 1981, it established the Education and Community Resources (EDCORE) Program that funds selected projects in partnership with local IP manufacturing facilities. In Kaukauna, Wisconsin, for example, EDCORE and IP's Thilmany mill organized a home remodel-

ing project that gave at-risk students opportunities to gain hands-on experience in building construction. In Jay, Maine, where IP operates the Androscoggin mill, EDCORE provided funding for a school and community recycling program. Also in the late 1980s, the Foundation established the Volunteers of International Paper (VIP) Program. The purpose of the VIP Fund is to recognize efforts of International Paper employees. The Foundation provides up to $500 in grant funds to non-profit organizations for specific projects. During the 1990s, the Foundation's focus has been in the area of education; health and welfare; arts and culture; environment; and community and civic organizations.

INTERNATIONAL PAPER REALTY

Begun in 1974, International Paper Realty identifies land in International Paper's timberland holdings that has uses more valuable than timber. IP Realty then purchases this land in bulk from the company, and sells it to developers and private contractors in smaller tracts. IP Realty sold nearly 300,000 acres of timberland from 1974 to 1997.

IP Realty owned, or helped develop, ski communities at Killington and Stratton, Vermont; an oceanfront development at Litchfield-by-the-Sea, South Carolina; and a golf community at Haig Point on Daufuskie Island, South Carolina.

KIPAWA, QUEBEC PULP MILL

The Kipawa mill, located in Temiskaming, Quebec, was built in 1920 by the Riordon Company, Ltd., a Canadian company established in 1857. Kipawa was the first mill in North America designed and equipped for dissolving woodpulps.

In 1925, International Paper acquired Riordon and integrated Kipawa into Canadian International Paper, its new subsidiary. In 1929, expansion of the mill brought production levels to 300 tons per day. In 1964, a crude alcohol plant was installed to produce alcohol out of sulfite waste liquor. By 1969, annual production of dissolving sulfite pulp reached 150,000 tons. Kipawa was shut down and later sold in the 1970s.

Kipawa mill

KRAFT PAPER AND PAPERBOARD

Bag for insulation packaging

"Kraft" is a Swedish and German word for "strength." Made from sulfate pulp, kraft paper is a tough grade used in a variety of products, especially bags and linerboard.

The sulfate pulp process was developed in 1883 and first introduced in Scandinavian mills to make kraft wrapping paper. It arrived in the United States in 1910 and was commercialized in Northern mills, including a small plant at Van Buren, Maine, that was acquired by International Paper in 1919.

In the South, kraft papermaking prospered after an American inventor discovered a process that made the region's heavily resinated woods suitable for pulping. The kraft mill which began operations in 1913 in Moss Point, Mississippi — one of the first in the South — was later acquired by International Paper. In 1921, the Bastrop Pulp and Paper Company completed a kraft mill at Bastrop, Louisiana, that produced bag and wrapping grades. IP became active in Southern kraft production when it acquired the Bastrop mill in 1925. Two years later, it entered the kraft conversion business with the acquisition of the George & Sherrard Paper Company of Wellsburg, West Virginia, a small producer of multiwall bags.

IP increased its presence in Southern kraft during the late 1920s with the construction of new mills in Camden, Arkansas; Mobile, Alabama; and Panama City, Florida. Simultaneously, it phased out its small Northern kraft operations. In 1931, IP made the first kraft linerboard on the Fourdrinier machine at Panama City, Florida. Prior to this breakthrough, kraft linerboard was made on cylinder machines that had the capacity to process this heavyweight grade.

Fourdrinier machines ran three times faster than cylinder machines and used 30 percent less fiber. IP later introduced the technology at its existing kraft mills and at new mills in Georgetown, South Carolina, and Springhill, Louisiana. Kraft linerboard products introduced by IP during these years included Gator Hide®, a grade widely used in shipping containers.

The next step in the development of kraft paper was the introduction of bleached grades. Early kraft paper had a characteristic brown color that can be seen in today's unbleached grades. Pulpmakers later developed a continuous bleaching process that was adopted by IP during the 1930s. In 1934, the Moss Point, Mississippi, mill installed a bleach plant. Four years later, the Springhill, Louisiana, mill produced the first bleached kraft paperboard on the Fourdrinier machine for conversion into milk containers, folding cartons, file folders, tag paper and similar items.

The introduction of bleached grades opened new markets for kraft paperboard. One of IP's largest customers for bleached grades was Single Service Containers, Inc., a pioneer maker of paper milk cartons, that was acquired by IP in 1946. Bleached grades were also used by folding carton and label producers such as Lord Baltimore Press, acquired by IP in 1958.

By the 1950s, the basic kraft process was in place and the rate of innovation slowed. Most subsequent work involved new applications of existing technology. International Paper's Erling Riis Research Laboratory at Mobile, Alabama, for example, used the kraft process to produce Acetakraft®, an acetate dissolving pulp manufactured on a commercial scale at the Natchez, Mississippi, mill in 1968 for producers of acetate textiles and cigarette filters.

KWIDZYN, POLAND PULP AND PAPER MILL

Acquired by International Paper in 1992, Poland's Kwidzyn mill near Gdansk is the largest integrated bleached paper mill in Central Europe.

Kwidzyn was built by the Polish government from 1982 to 1985. Design and construction were entrusted to H. A. Simons, a Canadian engineering firm that outfitted it with state-of-the-art technology. The vast Kwidzyn complex featured bleach pulp plants and four large paper machines that produced printing, writing, newsprint and linerboard grades.

After the collapse of communism, Poland sold Kwidzyn to International Paper for $150 million in 1992. During the next several years, IP invested $175 million in a modernization program that included a complete overhaul of the production equipment as well as worker training. The goal of the new investment was to increase annual production capacity from 217,000 to 400,000 metric tons. During the upgrade, Kwidzyn's papermakers worked closely with IP experts and Aussedat Rey, IP's French subsidiary. While the bulk of Kwidzyn's newsprint output is purchased by Polish customers, 40 percent of its uncoated white paper is sold in western European markets.

LINERBOARD AND CORRUGATED CONTAINERS

A corrugated container consists of two sheets of linerboard with a wavy sheet of corrugating medium sandwiched in between.

The development of corrugating medium preceded that of linerboard. The first commercially successful product was invented by Albert L. Jones, who obtained a U.S. patent in 1871. Early corrugating medium was an unlined material that was wrapped around glass and other fragile items shipped in wooden crates. The first corrugated boxes were made in 1894 at a mill in Schuylersville, New York. Most shells were made from jute and straw board well into the 1930s, when the widespread introduction of kraft linerboard transformed the corrugated container industry.

Kraft linerboard was made from sulfate pulp, consisting of long, strong fibers. Early kraft technology originated in Scandinavia and received further development in the United States, when an American inventor produced sulfate kraft pulp using Southern pinewood. Kraft linerboard was first produced on a commercial scale in 1923 on cylinder machines and started to replace jute and strawboard as a shell material for corrugated containers.

IP started kraft linerboard production on Fourdrinier machines in 1931, when its subsidiary Southern Kraft Corporation opened a new mill at Panama City, Florida. Fourdriniers produced kraft linerboard at 1,500 feet per minute, three times faster than cylinder machines. During the 1930s, Panama City and other IP linerboard mills supplied the Agar Manufacturing Corporation, a leading producer of corrugated containers, with plants in Somerville, Massachusetts; Whippany, New Jersey; Chicago, Illinois; and Kansas City, Kansas. IP acquired Agar in 1940 and thus became the nation's first paper company to integrate the production of kraft linerboard and corrugated containers.

In 1944, Agar was renamed IP Container Corporation, which developed a series of new products, including the first corrugated box for major appliances, customized containers for textile and synthetic rubber products and corrugated boxes for citrus fruit. Also during the 1940s, IP developed a new corrugating medium named Chem Fibre® that was made from hardwood pulp and first produced at the Bastrop mill in Louisiana.

The Container Division forged a strong relationship with the poultry industry by developing a series of innovative corrugated containers. The first was a wax-impregnated, curtain-coated box introduced in the early 1960s. Later breakthroughs included Classic Pak®, which enabled IP to capture 30 percent of the poultry packaging market in the 1990s.

Other important customers were produce packaging firms. To meet the needs of this market, IP introduced the Surf-Corr™ container for ice-packed fresh produce in 1971. The rigid-when-wet Surf-Corr box was especially popular in California, where it was used to ship wet-packed produce to the East Coast. IP later followed up with a triple-strength box made of specially treated corrugated board that provided high-compression strength and stackability for produce in high-humidity, cold storage.

The Container Division offered customers a variety of support services to enhance packaging systems. It operated an equipment development laboratory in Westfield, Massachusetts, that designed and constructed packaging machinery for customers.

During the 1970s, IP manufactured linerboard at its mills in Georgetown, South Carolina; Panama City, Florida; Vicksburg, Mississippi; and Gardiner, Oregon. Corrugating medium, made from stiff-fibered hardwood pulp, was manufactured at IP mills in Bastrop, Louisiana, and Georgetown, South Carolina. To improve corrugating medium production, IP developed green liquor pulping that used green liquor derived from the kraft process.

Rising production costs during the late 1970s triggered significant changes on the production side. The Panama City mill was sold in 1979, Bastrop closed in 1982 and Georgetown converted from linerboard to

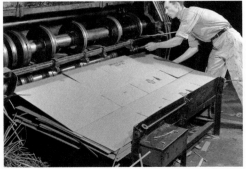

Corrugated container manufacturing

bleached products. But the completion of IP's new Mansfield, Louisiana, mill in 1981 reinvigorated containerboard production. Mansfield began production in 1981 with an annual capacity of 460,000 tons of linerboard and 270,000 tons of corrugating medium. Together with mills in Pineville, Louisiana; Vicksburg, Mississippi; and Gardiner, Oregon, Mansfield helped IP reduce its production costs significantly.

The division was strengthened further with the conversion of the Oswego, New York, mill to recycled linerboard in the early 1990s. In the mid-1990s, the company enhanced its position in corrugated container recycling with the construction of a third paper machine at Mansfield which produced lightweight linerboard and white top printing grades from recovered fiber.

Facility Location	Year built/ acquired		Facility Location	Year built/ acquired
Kansas City, Kansas #	1940		Las Palmas, Canary Islands	1966
Sommerville, Massachusetts #	1940		Detroit, Michigan	1967
Whippany, New Jersey #	1940		Murfreesboro, Tennessee	1968
Georgetown, South Carolina	1942		Modesto, California	1969
St. Louis, Missouri #	1946		Tallman, New York •	1969
Springhill, Louisiana	1946		Bilbao, Spain*	1970
Commerce, California #	1947		Creil, France*	1970
Wooster, Ohio	1948		Minneapolis, Minnesota	1970
Manchester, New Hampshire*	1953		Putnam, Connecticut	1972
Geneva, New York	1955		Barcelona, Spain*	1973
Edinburg, Texas	1957		Bellusco, Italy*	1974
Houston, Texas #	1957		Pedemonte, Italy*	1974
San Jose, California #	1957		Winsford, United Kingdom*	1974
Auburndale, Florida	1958		San Felice, Italy*	1974
Fond du Lac, Wisconsin	1958		Russellville, Arkansas	1975
Mason, Ohio	1958		Valladolid, Spain*	1976
Fresno, California #	1959		Bayamon, Puerto Rico #	1977
Philadelphia, Pennsylvania #	1959		Carson, California*	1980
Omaha, Nebraska #	1960		Chantilly, France	1981
Phoenix, Arizona #	1960		Stockbridge, Georgia #	1981
Chicago, Illinois	1961		Shreveport, Louisiana	1986
Pomezia, Italy	1961		Stockton, California #	1986
Pittsburgh, Pennsylvania #	1962		El Paso, Texas*	1987
Presque Isle, Maine #	1962		Chalon-sur-Saone, France*	1991
Statesville, North Carolina	1962		LePuy, France*	1991
Catania, Italy*	1963		Mount Carmel, Pennsylvania*	1992
Dallas, Texas	1963		Delavan, Wisconsin	1993
Arles, France*	1964		Suva, Fiji*	1995
Mortagne, France*	1964			
Bay Minette, Alabama	1965		* acquired	
Guadeloupe, French West Indies	1965		# closed	
Baltimore, Maryland #	1966		• sold	

LIQUID PACKAGING

Liquid packaging was dominated by glass and metal products until the 1930s, when the Pure Pak® milk carton was introduced. Pioneering work was done by the Ex-Cell-O Corporation, a Detroit precision machine tool manufacturer, which completed the first waxed milk carton machine in 1936. To reduce space and freight costs, Ex-Cell-O supplied dairies with flat paperboard blanks instead of fully assembled cartons. At the dairy, the Ex-Cell-O machine folded the blanks into cartons, which were then waxed, filled and sealed in a single operation. American consumers bought 42 million paper milk cartons during the first year, making Pure Pak an instant success.

In 1937, Ex-Cell-O licensed three paper companies to produce carton blanks. One of these licenses was soon acquired by Single Service Containers, a small company with a plant in Chelsea, Massachusetts. Grappling with production problems, Single Service Containers experimented with a variety of paperboard types and in 1939 settled on a bleached kraft grade produced at IP's Springhill, Louisiana mill. The Springhill mill was the first to produce suitable paperboard on the paper machine for milk carton blanks.

International Paper acquired Single Service Containers in 1946 to improve its position in paper conversion and provide an outlet for its growing bleached kraft production capacities. Initially operating as a wholly owned subsidiary, Single Service Containers became an IP division in 1948 and was renamed the Liquid Packaging Division in 1979. During the 1950s, IP improved the waxed Pure Pak carton by switching from lithographic printing to flexographic printing that produced superior graphics and more colorful cartons. It also introduced the Pitcher-Pour® spout which replaced the lift tab. These innovations decreased production costs and increased consumer acceptance of the waxed Pure Pak carton which became a standard household item in the 1950s.

International Paper's liquid packaging operations made a quantum leap in technology with the switch from wax to plastic-coated cartons. In 1955, IP launched a multimillion dollar research program to develop a polyethylene-coated carton in cooperation with university researchers, Ex-Cell-O and leading plastics manufacturers, such as DuPont and Union Carbide. With the basic product in place by the late 1950s, International Paper installed polymer extruders to apply polyethylene to paperboard at its mills in Mobile, Alabama, and Niagara Falls, New York. This also required new printing and sealing techniques to be developed. Ex-Cell-O meanwhile converted 3,200 wax filling machines to the plastic coated method. The polyethylene-coated carton finally went into commercial production in 1960, enhancing IP's position as the nation's leading milk carton producer. Liquid packaging board was by now produced at several mills, including the Pine Bluff, Arkansas, mill (1957) and a new mill in Texarkana, Texas, which began operation in 1972.

Meanwhile, the Liquid Packaging Division and IP researchers continued to improve the Pure Pak carton. During the 1960s, the Erling Riis Research Laboratory in Mobile, Alabama, developed a foil-laminated carton featuring superior barrier properties. This product went into commercial production at the Pine Bluff, Arkansas, mill in 1965 and replaced glass jugs as the leading container for soft drink syrups. Extrusion coating and foil lamination produced technological spin-offs during the 1970s, when the Erling Riis Research Laboratory and IP's new Corporate Research Center in Sterling Forest, New York, developed Pressware® and Oven-Pak®, polyester-coated paperboard food containers that were suitable for both conventional and microwave ovens.

During the 1980s, IP's Liquid Packaging Division marketed a variety of new barrier boards resistant to the passage of organic flavor molecules. Resulting in Barrier Board™

and Barrier Pak®, these products became the catalyst to grow and improve the Ready to Serve (RTS) market. This was followed in the 1990s by Spout-Pak®, a pouring closure device for gabletop cartons providing more utility, sealability and product freshness for both juice and milk. IP now produces liquid packaging cartons in 22 facilities in 11 countries around the world. Using flexographic, lithographic and rotogravure printing for the dairy, juice and aseptic and specialty markets, IP is truly the world's leader in liquid packaging.

Facility Location	Year built/ acquired
Atlanta, Georgia	1951
Kansas City, Kansas	1951
Kalamazoo, Michigan	1952
Youngstown, Ohio#	1953
Minneapolis, Minnesota#	1955
Philadelphia, Pennsylvania	1955
Raleigh, North Carolina	1957
Turlock, California	1957
Caracas, Venezuela	1959
Miami, Florida#	1959
Framingham, Massachusetts	1960
Versailles, Kentucky#	1960
Longview, Washington#	1962
Los Angeles, California#	1965
Tallman, New York#	1969
Tokyo, Japan	1976
Edmonton, Alberta, Canada	1979
Santiago, Dominican Republic	1980
Perugia, Italy	1981
Taipei, Taiwan	1983
Seoul, Korea	1984
Longueuil, Quebec, Canada*	1989
Cedar Rapids, Iowa*	1991
Kingston, Jamaica	1991
London, Ontario, Canada	1991
Plant City, Florida	1992
Itu, Brazil	1994
St. Priest, France	1996
San Salvador, El Salvador	1997

* acquired

\# closed

LOCK HAVEN, PENNSYLVANIA PAPER MILL

Opened in 1880, the Lock Haven mill in central Pennsylvania was initially known as the Pennsylvania Pulp and Paper Company. Ten years later, the name was changed to the New York and Pennsylvania Company as a result of a merger. In 1950, the mill was acquired by the Curtis Publishing Company and began producing paper for magazines such as *The Saturday Evening Post* and *The Ladies' Home Journal*. In 1965, the mill was purchased by the Hammermill Paper Company. Production shifted to fine papers, and later to copier and commercial printing papers. The Lock Haven mill joined International Paper when Hammermill was acquired in 1986.

Over the past decade, the mill has pioneered new grades, including Hammermill Laser Print and Jet Print products, which have helped build the market for ink and laser jet printers. In 1993, a de-inking and recycling plant was built to turn old newspapers and magazines into pulp for copier and commercial printing grades. The market for this 100 percent recycled paper failed to materialize and the operation was discontinued in 1997.

Today, Lock Haven operates five paper machines and five sheet converting units, producing nearly 700 tons a day. The mill continues to invest in new product and packaging innovations, including the installation in 1998 of a new retail packaging line to meet customer needs in the small office and home office sectors.

Lock Haven mill

LONG-BELL LUMBER CORPORATION

A manufacturer of building products with extensive production facilities and timber holdings, Long-Bell Lumber Corporation was acquired by International Paper in 1956 and was later integrated into IP's wood products business.

Long-Bell was founded almost by accident in 1875, when Richard Long, a struggling entrepreneur, sold lumber salvaged from his bankrupt hay business and to his own surprise made a profit. Looking for an opportunity to start a new business, Long opened a lumber yard in Columbus, Ohio, that evolved into the Long-Bell Lumber Company, incorporated in 1885.

Long-Bell built its first lumber mill in 1890 at Antlers, Oklahoma, and acquired its first timberlands in 1896 near Thomasville, Oklahoma. Several new mills built during subsequent years included a facility completed in 1903 at DeRidder, Louisiana.

Headquartered in Kansas City, Kansas, Long-Bell expanded to the West Coast beginning in 1904. By the 1920s, it was one of the nation's largest producers of plywood, hardwood lumber and building products. During the Great Depression, Long-Bell teetered on the brink of bankruptcy, but the company recovered during the economic boom of World War II.

When IP announced its decision to acquire Long-Bell with its extensive timberlands and wood products operations in 1956, the Federal Trade Commission launched an anti-trust investigation. At that time, IP was already three times larger than its closest competitor, and the FTC argued that the Long-Bell acquisition would impair free com-

petition in the paper and wood products sectors. To appease federal regulators, IP promised not to acquire a major competitor over the next 10 years. The Long-Bell acquisition was completed in 1957.

Long-Bell operated as an IP division for several years and in 1960 completed a new plywood and lumber center in Chelatchie, Washington. It was later integrated into International Paper's Wood Products Division.

LORD BALTIMORE PRESS

One of the leading American folding carton producers after World War II, Lord Baltimore Press was acquired by International Paper in 1958 and became a building block for its folding carton operations.

The company, founded in 1875 as the Friedenwald Company of Baltimore, initially specialized in book printing by letterpress, and changed its name to Lord Baltimore Press at the turn of the century. Diversifying into lithographic printing for folding cartons during the 1920s, it became the first in the industry to operate four-, five- and six-color offset presses. It also developed an innovative lithographic process to reproduce fine-screen illustrations on boxboard.

Still operating as Lord Baltimore Press following its acquisition by International Paper, LBP opened a new plant in Clinton, Iowa, in 1958, and started a folding carton facility in Cincinnati, Ohio, in 1962. It was integrated into IP's new Folding Carton and Label Division in December 1972.

LOUISIANA PULP AND PAPER MILL, BASTROP, LOUISIANA

Constructed in 1924 under the supervision of Richard Cullen and Erling Riis, the Louisiana mill at Bastrop was the second mill in the area; its companion, the Bastrop mill, had been built several years earlier. The Louisiana mill opened in 1925 with two paper machines that produced 100 tons of kraft paper daily. It was acquired by IP in 1927. The No. 3 machine went into production in 1948.

To supplement its kraft paper manufacturing operations, Louisiana built a converting plant that produced grocery bags in 1928.

When grocery bag production was transferred to the Mobile mill, Louisiana's converting plant switched to multiwall sacks.

After World War II, another converting plant was built by the Single Service Division which produced paper milk cartons. In 1955, the mill commercialized a low-wax milk carton stock that cut wax board consumption by 50 percent. It also developed punch card stock for early IBM computers.

The late 1960s marked the beginning of a new chapter in the Louisiana mill's history. During an extensive reconfiguration, the mill added a new recovery boiler and additional pulp cooking and storage capacity. Its No. 3 machine was shut down, disassembled and transferred to IP's new Texarkana, Texas, mill, where it started up as the No. 2 machine in 1972. The Louisiana mill replaced it with a new No. 3 machine producing uncoated white paper. It also converted some of its kraft paper capacity to bleached printing and business grades that enabled it to enter new markets. The investment paid off during the 1970s and 1980s, when printing papers commanded a better price than kraft grades as a result of broad changes in demand.

MANSFIELD, LOUISIANA PULP AND PAPER MILL

The construction of International Paper's Mansfield, Louisiana, containerboard mill from 1979 to 1981 was part of a plan to modernize the company's manufacturing base. The industry's largest and most advanced low-cost mill, Mansfield began production in 1981 with two paper machines that produced 460,000 tons per year of linerboard and 270,000 tons of corrugating medium. The mill received a significant amount of raw material from recently acquired timberlands in Louisiana, purchased from the Bodcaw Company. The mill also processed wood chips from IP's new plywood and lumber manufacturing plant at Springhill, Louisiana.

In 1994, Mansfield launched a plant improvement program that added a third containerboard machine with an annual capacity of 400,000 tons. This $300 million investment program also gave the mill a recycling plant that processed old corrugated containers at a rate of 1,300 tons per day. Recognizing the mill's outstanding safety record, the Occupational Safety and Health Administration (OSHA) presented Mansfield with its highest award for workplace safety in 1994, the first given to any IP mill. Mansfield produces perhaps the widest range of linerboard and medium products in the industry. Linerboard products include Pineliner® high performance, Hydrokraft® wet strength and White Top® grades.

MASONITE CORPORATION

William H. Mason, an associate of Thomas A. Edison, founded the Mason Fibre Company in 1925. Mason's revolutionary discovery that waste wood chips, until this time used only as a source of fuel, could be exploded into a soft, fluffy material eventually led to the creation of Masonite® Hardboard. The Mason Fibre Company, as it was known until 1928, became the world's first hardboard manufacturer.

Mason's process was the first to break down wood and put it back together in thin, tough sheets using only the natural binders of wood to hold the fibers together. A patent issued on the process in 1933 allowed newcomer Masonite to force more established competitors such as Celotex and National Gypsum to become its agents for selling Masonite products. That same year, Masonite introduced its Century of Progress flooring at the Chicago World's Fair.

By the early 1950s, cheaper methods of producing a product similar to Masonite Hardboard had eroded the company's market share. Masonite recognized the need to produce a new family of hardboard products, much as traditional paper companies had earlier branched out into specialty paper products. A number of new products introduced in the 1950s helped Masonite expand its consumer base. These included Benelex®— used mainly for dies in nonferrous metal-forming for airplane manufacture; Misty Walnut—interior paneling that was neither "misty" nor "walnut," but sold in the millions of feet; and "X"— a weatherproof hardboard for exterior use. The introduction of a variety of products with differing colors, patterns, shapes, textures, grains and laminates further diversified the company's product line.

Beginning in the 1940s, Masonite made several acquisitions, including Marsh Wall Products, James Seeman Studios, Peg Board®, and Thrasher Lumber Co. The company also purchased large tracts of forest, primarily in Mississippi. International expansion was an important part of Masonite's growth, initially in Sweden in 1928, and eventually with the creation of companies in Australia, Italy, South Africa and Canada. The Canadian interest was a joint venture in 1939 with Canadian International Paper.

During the 1980s, an adverse business climate and a lack of new product development nearly caused Masonite to cease operations. In 1988, the company was purchased by International Paper. New products, such as molded doorfacing panels, have revitalized Masonite and expanded International Paper's wood products operations.

Facility Location	Year built
Lisbon Falls, Maine	1889
Laurel, Mississippi	1925
Ukiah, California	1950
Pilot Rock, Oregon	1953
West Chicago, Illinois	1960
Towanda, Pennsylvania	1965
Danville, Virginia	1965
Cordele, Georgia	1990
Carrick-on-Shannon, Ireland	1996
Durban, Republic of South Africa	1949

MILLERS FALLS, MASSACHUSETTS PAPER MILL

The Millers Falls mill was owned by the Strathmore Paper Company and later became a part of International Paper's fine papers operations.

The mill was built in 1902 by the Millers Falls Paper Company. Operating two Fourdrinier machines that produced high-quality bond and writing grades, it competed with Strathmore in the market for correspondence paper until 1982, when Strathmore acquired Millers Falls. A plant modernization program increased the capacity of the No. 1 machine by 50 percent and improved the speed performance of the No. 2 machine.

MUIRSON LABEL COMPANY

Founded in 1913, the Muirson Label Company was a leading carton and label producer based in San Jose, California. It was acquired by International Paper in 1960 as part of a long-term strategy to increase IP's converting capabilities. Manufacturing operations at the time of the acquisition included plants in San Jose, California; Peoria, Illinois; and Meriden, Connecticut.

Muirson Label remained a separate subsidiary of IP until 1973 when it was combined with the Lord Baltimore Press to form International Paper's Folding Carton and Label Division.

During subsequent years, label manufacturing facilities were closed and International Paper consolidated label operations at a new facility in Bowling Green, Kentucky.

MOBILE, ALABAMA PULP AND PAPER MILL

International Paper's Mobile mill, located near extensive timberland acquired by the company in the 1920s, was built in 1928 and turned up its first reel of paper on September 23, 1929. Originally equipped with two machines, Mobile later installed two Fourdriniers that had been transferred from two Northeastern mills which had ceased operations. Machines No. 1 and 2 produced bag and wrapping grades. Machines No. 3 and 4, which were equipped with Yankee dryers, made glazed bleached and unbleached kraft paper. The mill received a power plant and a recovery boiler in 1941, followed by a second recovery boiler five years later.

The mill subsequently became the center of the Southern Kraft Division, whose headquarters were located in Mobile. The mill received a $43 million upgrade that added two paper machines, six digesters, a sheet finishing department and a polyethylene extruder in 1957. The No. 5 machine was the first to produce Southern newsprint. As part of the 1957 upgrade, the No. 2 machine was converted from kraft grades to lightweight bleached papers made from 100 percent hardwood pulp—the first fine business grades produced in the South. By the late 1950s, Mobile was one of the most advanced mills in the industry, with a daily output of 500 tons.

During the 1960s and 1970s, several upgrades increased the mill's capacity to 1,300 tons and replaced two older recovery boilers with a more modern unit that had a daily capacity of 700 tons.

In the early 1980s, IP launched an extensive mill reconfiguration program. The conversion of the No. 5 machine from newsprint to printing and writing papers, for example, was part of IP's strategic effort to reduce its presence in the poorly performing newsprint market and enter high-value product lines. Also part of the reconfiguration was the conversion of the No. 6 machine from kraft paper to printing and writing grades. The No. 1 paper machine was taken out of service in 1997.

Mobile became a leading producer of printing and bag grades in the 1990s. Continuing a long tradition of environmental stewardship, the mill converted a former wasteland area into a protected wetland and wildlife preserve that received IP's Environmental Award of Excellence in 1994.

MOSS POINT, MISSISSIPPI PULP AND PAPER MILL

Moss Point, one of the first Southern paper mills, was acquired by International Paper in 1928, to increase Southern kraft production capabilities. Its original owner, the Southern Paper Company, built the mill in 1912 to manufacture heavy fiber and wrapping paper. Operations started on July 1, 1913, with two paper machines. Initially, the mill processed residuals from local sawmills, but later switched to pine pulpwood to manufacture kraft paper. A remodeling program, begun in 1922, increased the mill's daily output from 40 to 100 tons. The No. 3 machine went on stream in 1924.

During the Great Depression, the mill shut down for extended periods of time because of a lack of orders. To reposition the mill in the paper market, IP installed a bleach plant in August 1934, enabling Moss Point to produce bleached kraft wrapping and specialty papers.

In 1936, the mill installed the No. 4 paper machine; this unit was transferred from IP's defunct Rumford, Maine, mill and increased Moss Point's daily output capacity to 250 tons. The bleach plant made history the same year when it became the first IP mill to commercialize the continuous bleaching method that replaced the batch processes. In 1950, Moss Point installed the No. 5 paper machine, a bleached kraft unit with a daily capacity of 500 tons that went on stream in 1951. Accounting for 60 percent of the mill's output, the No. 5 machine received a coater in 1955 that applied clay coating to create a bright finish. The No. 5 machine later received the mill's first paper machine computer.

Responding to a decline in demand for uncoated board grades, Moss Point phased out machines No. 1 and No. 4 in 1973, leaving three Fourdriniers whose main output was high-quality coated board and label stock. New environmental technology installed during this period included a non-condensable gas collection system and a secondary wastewater treatment system. A large recovery boiler received major upgrades in 1979 and 1987.

New initiatives followed during the 1990s. Building on earlier efforts to improve environmental standards, Moss Point became the first IP mill to introduce Elemental Chlorine Free bleaching in 1993.

Four years later, the mill shut down the No. 2 paper machine, which had been installed in 1912 as one of Moss Point's first machines. Lloyd's Register Quality Assurance approved Moss Point's No. 5 paper machine for ISO certification in 1996, followed by No. 3 and an off-machine coater a year later. To earn certification, the mill had to docu-

Moss Point mill

ment and implement a quality system that conformed to the requirements of the ISO 9002 quality standard.

NATCHEZ, MISSISSIPPI PULP MILL

International Paper built the Natchez, Mississippi, mill in 1950 to manufacture dissolving pulp. The process of manufacturing dissolving pulp using Southern hardwoods was developed at the initiative of Erling Riis, then vice president and general manager of the Southern Kraft Division, and John Gilbert, a senior research scientist. Initially, dissolving pulp was used by producers of rayon, tire cords, cellophane and plastics.

Natchez began production in January 1951 and was an immediate success. Three months later, IP announced that capacity would be doubled. In 1958, Natchez installed a chemical post-treatment process developed at IP's research laboratory in

Mobile, Alabama, that enhanced the purity of dissolving pulp.

When demand for rayon pulp declined in the late 1960s, Natchez switched to Acetakraft®, an acetate dissolving pulp that was used to manufacture acetate, textiles and cigarette filters. In 1974, the mill installed a new $21 million recovery boiler and an advanced black liquor oxidation system. Further updating its boiler equipment, it built a new power bark boiler in 1981 that used bark, fossil fuels and waste treatment by-product as energy sources. During the 1980s, Natchez introduced the operator concept, in which all employees acquired greater decision-making authority.

Natchez mill

NEWSPRINT

Once International Paper's main product, newsprint is an inexpensive printing paper used by newspapers. Modern newsprint production started in 1867 with the introduction of groundwood pulp, an inexpensive material first made in the United States by Albrecht Pagenstecher, who built what later became IP's Hudson River mill. Combined with small amounts of higher-quality pulp that added strength, groundwood pulp produced a cost-efficient paper that quickly replaced the more expensive all-rag newsprint grades. Wood-based newsprint production skyrocketed during the 1880s and 1890s, leading to overcapacity. To help stabilize the industry, 17 paper mills pooled their resources in 1898 to form International Paper.

The world's largest newsprint producer at the turn of the century, IP supplied newspapers in the United States and overseas, including *The New York Times*, *The Chicago Tribune* and *La Prenza*, Latin America's largest daily, published in Buenos Aires. In 1913, however, Congress lifted tariffs on inexpensive Canadian newsprint, triggering the industry's decline in the United States. Over the next three decades, IP converted its Northeastern mills to book grades and transferred newsprint production to Canada. The company acquired extensive woodlands and, in 1925, formed Canadian International Paper, a wholly owned subsidiary operating the world's largest newsprint mills.

The key to successful newsprint production was inexpensive groundwood pulp, which was readily available in Canada with its vast softwood resources. In the United States, the IP research laboratory at Mobile, Alabama, developed a pulping method for Southern pine, which had previously not been used for newsprint production. The technique was first commercialized at the Mobile, Alabama, mill, which produced pine-based newsprint beginning in 1957. The Pine Bluff, Arkansas, mill used the same technique beginning in 1958.

Always subject to extreme fluctuations, the American newsprint market entered a period of decline in the 1970s. In response, IP sold its Canadian operations in 1981 for $900 million and invested the proceeds in a large-scale overhaul of its U.S. mills. As part of a mill reconfiguration program in the mid-1980s, IP phased out newsprint production at Mobile and Pine Bluff and started producing other grades. But the company's withdrawal from the newsprint business was only temporary. In 1992, IP acquired the Kwidzyn mill in Poland, which included a newsprint machine that supplied European markets.

NIAGARA FALLS, NEW YORK PULP AND PAPER MILL

Niagara Falls was one of the 17 mills that pooled their resources to form International Paper in 1898. Equipped with six paper machines, eight wood grinders and six sulfite digesters, the mill produced a daily output of 150 tons of newsprint. Extensive reconstruction became necessary when a fire destroyed parts of the physical plant in 1917.

Like other newsprint mills in IP's Northern operations, Niagara Falls was unable to compete with inexpensive Canadian producers and hence converted to sulfite bond and book grades in 1919. During the conversion process, the mill also built company-owned homes that comprised the LaSalle housing complex. Many of these homes were later sold to local mill employees.

Later additions to the mill enabled it to produce high-grade kraft specialty papers. Despite a number of improvements, the Niagara Falls mill was unable to compete long term and was closed in 1967.

Niagara Falls mill

NICOLET PAPER COMPANY, DePERE WISCONSIN

The history of the Nicolet Paper Company goes back to 1892, when the Shattuck and Babcock Company, a subsidiary of what was then Kimberly-Clark and Company, built a two-machine paper mill in De Pere, Wisconsin. Located in the Fox River Valley, the plant had a daily capacity of 20 tons and produced expensive, rag-content writing grades. The economic depression of 1893 reduced demand for high-quality papers, compelling the owners to sell the mill to the American Writing Paper Company in 1899. Struggling to stay afloat during the early 20th century, the mill closed temporarily in 1922.

A group of Wisconsin industrialists acquired the De Pere plant in 1927 and reopened it as the Nicolet Paper Company, which derived its name from a European explorer who had visited the Fox River Valley in the 17th century. Reconfiguring the mill, the new owners switched from writing grades to wood-based glassine and grease-proof papers which were used as a packaging material for candy bars, cereals and potato chips during the 1930s. Philip Morris, Inc., acquired the mill in the mid-1950s and sold it to the Hammermill Paper Company in 1985. One year later, Hammermill and its subsidiaries were acquired by International Paper. In the 1990s, Nicolet produced mostly backing papers for pressure sensitive labels and tapes.

NORTHERN DIVISION

Together with the Southern Kraft Division, the Northern Division was one of International Paper's two main manufacturing divisions before 1976.

The foundations for the Northern Division were laid in 1898, when 17 mills in New York and New England merged to form International Paper. When the company built up its Southern kraft and Canadian newsprint operations during the 1920s and 1930s, the Northeastern mills were consolidated into the Northern Division with headquarters in Glens Falls, New York. In addition to overseeing the mills, most of which specialized in printing grades, the division was responsible for woodlands management in Maine, New Hampshire, Vermont and New York. In 1964, its Northeastern mills were joined by IP's new linerboard mill at Gardiner, Oregon.

The Northern Division was dissolved in 1976, when the company replaced its geographic divisions with product-based business units.

OSWEGO, NEW YORK PAPER MILL

The Oswego mill in upstate New York opened in 1927. Its first operator was the Taggert Oswego Paper and Bag Corporation, which produced heavy paper bags for cement, limestone and other dry materials. In 1951, the mill was sold to the Marathon Corporation which manufactured paperboard for products such as ice cream and frozen foods. In 1960, Oswego was acquired by the Hammermill Paper Company and converted to fine paper production. In 1963, Oswego started Hammermill's Papertronics Division, manufacturing small paper rolls used in cash registers and computer applications. These operations were phased out in 1982 because of poor earnings.

Oswego became part of IP with the acquisition of Hammermill in 1986. The mill was converted to recycled kraft production in the early 1990s and produced lightweight grades and Pineliner®, a high-performance grade.

OTIS PAPER MILL, LIVERMORE FALLS, MAINE

The Otis mill at Livermore Falls, Maine, was one of the 17 mills that joined in 1898 to form International Paper.

Otis was built in 1888 by Hugh Chisholm, owner of the Umbagog mill in nearby Livermore and later one of IP's founders. In the early 1900s, the mill operated nine paper machines and had a daily output of 200 tons of newsprint. An extensive plant improvement program, begun in 1904, increased newsprint production and added the No. 10 machine, which produced wrapping stock from waste paper collected throughout the mill. Otis received its pulp supplies from three IP groundwood mills in the vicinity: Falmouth, which fell victim to a disastrous fire in 1912; Livermore Falls; and Riley.

The Otis paper mill played an important role in the history of trade unionism at IP. In June 1902, local union representatives joined their counterparts from five other mills to sign the company's first contract with organized paperworkers.

The 1930s brought important changes in the mill's product mix. Like most mills in IP's Northern Division, Otis abandoned newsprint because it could no longer com-pete with inexpensive Canadian producers. The switch to groundwood specialty grades in 1935 and 1936 involved extensive changes in plant equipment, workforce retraining and a permanent shutdown of four obsolete machines. In 1938, operations were interrupted by extensive flooding that destroyed the mill dam.

In the years following the conversion, Otis produced a variety of specialty grades. In the 1960s, Otis produced coated paper for *Reader's Digest*, Alectric lightweight groundwood sheets for telephone directories and Elbar paper suitable for photocopiers.

The construction of IP's Androscoggin mill in the mid-1960s marked a turning point in the history of papermaking in the Jay area. Androscoggin, equipped with extensive pulping facilities, replaced Otis' former pulp suppliers. As a result, the Riley mill was phased out in 1965, followed by the Livermore Falls groundwood pulp mill in 1967. During subsequent years, Otis' machine Nos. 2, 3 and 10 were taken offline, but the remaining equipment received several upgrades. IP sold the Otis paper mill to the James River Company in 1978.

PANAMA CITY, FLORIDA PULP AND PAPER MILL

Originally designed to produce kraft wrapping paper, International Paper's facility at Panama City, Florida, started up in 1931 as a linerboard mill.

Panama City was built by the Southern Kraft Corporation (an IP subsidiary that was later renamed Southern Kraft Division) in an effort to expand its production base in the Southeast. The mill became the first to produce linerboard on the Fourdrinier machine, which ran faster and more efficiently than traditional cylinder machines. The bulk of its output was processed by corrugated container manufacturers. In 1937, IP's joint venture company, Arizona Chemical, opened a plant at Panama City that processed the paper mill's crude liquor turpentine, a by-product of the sulfate pulping method.

Using bleach technology developed at IP's Springhill mill in Louisiana, Panama City added a bleach plant and modified one of its paper machines in 1964. In addition to unbleached products and linerboard, Panama City began producing bleached market pulp and diaper pulp.

During the 1970s, the aging plant was unable to compete with newer mills in a stagnant economy. With investment capital tied up in other mill reconfiguration programs, IP decided that a large-scale modernization of Panama City was not feasible and sold the mill to Southwest Forest Industries in 1979.

PETROLEUM AND MINERALS

International Paper branched out into oil, gas, and minerals exploration in 1975, when it acquired General Crude Oil Company to explore for these products on company land.

Founded as a private partnership in 1921, General Crude was incorporated in 1933 in Houston, Texas. Over the years General Crude acquired a number of mineral properties including 55,000 acres of land just South of Houston, that continue to produce significant quantities of oil and gas. In partnership with other oil companies, General

Otis mill

Crude also explored for oil and natural gas resources in offshore fields near the Texas and Louisiana coast, as well as oil fields in Western states, the Rocky Mountains and Canada.

Attempts to locate oil on IP lands initially produced mixed results, but other activities earned profits. In 1979, IP sold the bulk of General Crude's oil and gas business to Mobil Oil Company for $763 million and used the proceeds to acquire the Bodcaw Company, which owned timberlands, minerals and a paper mill in Louisiana. After the sale to Mobil, IP's remaining petroleum and minerals activities were consolidated into GCO Minerals Company, which contin-

ued to manage and explore for minerals on IP lands throughout the United States.

In the mid-1980s, IP Petroleum Company, Inc. was formed. An ambitious exploration and development project in west Texas resulted in a significant IP Petroleum oil and gas discovery at Sugg Ranch near Midland. More than 700 wells are now in production as a result of this discovery alone.

IP Petroleum Company, Inc. and GCO Minerals Company, are collectively now referred to as the Petroleum and Minerals Division of International Paper, charged with mineral management responsibilities on IP lands where opportunities exist.

General Crude Oil off shore drilling rig

PINE BLUFF, ARKANSAS PULP AND PAPER MILL

Construction of the Pine Bluff, Arkansas, mill started on May 8, 1956, and the mill was fully operational in the summer of 1958. Initially, Pine Bluff produced newsprint and milk carton grades on two machines. It was the first mill to produce polyethylene coated milk carton stock, an innovative product that replaced wax-coated cartons and was developed in a joint research effort by International Paper, DuPont and Ex-Cell-O Corporation.

In 1960, Pine Bluff started its third paper machine for lightweight paper used in telephone directories. A multi-million dollar plant improvement program launched in the mid-1960s added automated digester facilities and improved woodyard and pulping operations. Pine Bluff scored another first in 1965, when it started commercial production of foil-laminated stock for Pure-Pak cartons. Developed at the Erling Riis Research Laboratory, this product was used by soft-drink manufacturers as a container for syrup.

The 1970s marked a difficult adjustment period. In 1974, the No. 3 machine was converted from lightweight grades and newsprint to recycled corrugated paper. The conversion was unsuccessful, forcing a return to newsprint in 1976. But a steep decline in the newsprint market compelled Pine Bluff to phase out newsprint production in 1984, leaving two of its three machines idle.

To avert a complete shutdown and to reposition Pine Bluff in the paper market, IP launched a $250 million plant improvement initiative that was part of the company's $6 billion capital expenditure. The No. 1 machine was converted to a state-of-the-art producer of coated publication grades. The No. 2 machine received an extensive upgrade that enhanced its ability to produce liquid packaging board. These improvements turned Pine Bluff into one of the most advanced manufacturers of coated board and publication papers in the 1990s.

PINEVILLE, LOUISIANA PULP AND PAPER MILL

Built by the Pineville Kraft Corporation, a joint venture of the Bodcaw Company and two European companies, the Pineville, Louisiana, mill began operating in August 1968 with one paper machine that produced unbleached kraft linerboard. Originally equipped for a capacity of 750 tons a day, Pineville started an expansion program in 1972 that added a press, 10 new dryers, new evaporator equipment and a second chip unloading system. These additions increased its capacity to nearly 900 tons per day, while later improvements increased output to 1,040 tons a day.

Bodcaw, which owned the 1,200 acre site where the mill was built, acquired full ownership of the Pineville Kraft Corporation in 1974. Five years later, when International Paper acquired Bodcaw, it added the mill to its containerboard operations. As part of a company-wide program to improve efficiency and product quality, Pineville installed a new step diffuser secondary headbox in 1983. Using long softwood fibers, it produced high-quality unbleached linerboard primarily for export markets.

A plant improvement completed in the early 1990s improved the purity and smoothness of Pineville's linerboard output. This enabled the mill to introduce ColorBrite® printing and coating liners, Pineliner® high ring crush linerboard and other high-quality grades. As IP's specialty linerboard mill, Pineville supplied the company's domestic containerboard plants and customers in the United States and overseas.

PRINTING AND WRITING PAPERS

Printing and writing papers are defined as papers used in business communication, envelopes, writing pads, file folders, books and magazines, etc.

Writing paper is the industry's oldest grade and was initially made from rag pulp to produce writing surfaces in ancient China and medieval Europe. Early printing papers, also derived from rag pulp, were introduced in the printing industry in the 15th century.

In the 19th century, demand for writing and printing papers increased as a growing percentage of the population became literate. Rag suppliers quickly became unable to meet demand for raw materials in the paper industry. Inexpensive and abundant groundwood pulp became available in the 1860s, but its use was limited to newsprint production because its inferior quality made it unsuitable for higher grades.

At the end of the 19th century, papermakers experimented with sulfite pulping methods that finally produced high-quality wood pulps for printing and writing grades. Pioneers included the Hammermill Paper Company in Erie, Pennsylvania, which produced sulfite-based writing paper that approached the quality of rag grades.

When International Paper was founded in 1898, some of its mills in New York and New England produced book and magazine paper. These switched to newsprint after the turn of the century because this product was considered more profitable. International Paper reconverted its Northern mills to writing and publication papers from the 1920s to the 1940s because they were unable to compete with inexpensive Canadian newsprint producers. The Hudson River mill in upstate New York, IP's last Northern mill to abandon newsprint, switched to printing grades in 1941 and soon carved out a specialty position in coated papers.

One of IP's most significant contributions to the industry was the introduction of hardwood pulps suitable for printing and writing paper production. Sulfite pulpers had traditionally used softwoods, which were scarcer and hence more expensive than hardwoods. A research initiative launched by IP's research laboratory at Mobile, Alabama, in the early 1950s used a chlorine dioxide bleaching method to produce 100 percent hardwood pulp. The technology was commercialized at the Mobile, Alabama, mill which converted its No. 2 machine to hardwood pulp-based printing papers in 1957. Although Mobile's 100 percent hardwood pulp remained rare, it paved the way for greater hardwood use in writing and printing paper production, enabling mills to use oak and other inexpensive species.

IP gradually expanded its printing and writing paper business during later years. In 1967, its new Androscoggin mill at Jay, Maine, started up one publication-grade machine, followed by a new machine for lightweight business papers at the Louisiana mill at Bastrop. In 1980, the Androscoggin mill converted its No. 2 machine from carbonizing tissue to publication grades. A capital expenditure launched in the early 1980s to increase production of high-value grades converted several machines to printing grades at Mobile, Alabama, and Georgetown, South Carolina.

Several acquisitions bolstered IP's presence in printing and writing papers. In 1986, IP acquired the Hammermill Paper Company, an industry leader with mills in Erie and Lock Haven, Pennsylvania; Millers Falls, Turners Falls and Woronoco, Massachusetts; Hamilton, Ohio; Selma, Alabama; and Oswego, New York. Three years later, IP acquired Germany's Zanders Feinpapiere AG and France's Aussedat Rey Company, both major producers of business grades. Adding to this production was the Kwidzyn mill in Poland—acquired in 1992 and the Tait mill in Scotland, acquired with the Federal Paper Board merger in 1996.

*Hammermill
Sample Pack*

QUALITY IMPROVEMENT PROCESS

The Quality Improvement Process (QIP) began in International Paper in 1984 with the establishment of a corporate goal, management principles and elements of quality improvement. QIP involved employees in running the business through membership in lead teams, area teams and task teams. The concept of internal customers helped people understand the impact their performance had on processes preceding and following their part of the operation. And, the concept of "quality" was broadened to include service, efficiency and involvement.

QIP gave employees greater influence on decision making at the production level. Drawing on employees' close familiarity with production and administrative processes, equipment and products, the program had produced thousands of initiatives by the 1990s.

RIEGELWOOD, NORTH CAROLINA PULP AND PAPER MILL

The Riegelwood mill was built in 1952 by the Riegel Paper Corporation, owner of several mills in the Northeastern states and extensive woodlands around the town of Riegelwood, North Carolina. Originally designated as a pulp mill with an annual capacity of 250,000 tons, Riegelwood installed its first Fourdrinier machine in 1958 to manufacture heavy paperboard, followed by a second machine in 1967 that produced lightweight paperboard grades.

During a subsequent slump in demand for paperboard, the Riegel Paper Company sold the mill, 350,000 acres of timberland and other operations for $115.6 million to the Federal Paper Board Company in 1972. Five years later, Federal started a $215 million modernization program that turned Riegelwood into the company's flagship mill and established it as the world's largest solid bleached sulfate pulp and paperboard mill.

In addition to light paperboard grades for posters and brochures, it produced market pulp for domestic and international customers. In 1996, Riegelwood became part of International Paper when the latter merged with the Federal Paper Board Company and integrated its operations.

RIVERDALE PULP AND PAPER MILL, SELMA, ALABAMA

The Riverdale mill is located near Selma in central Alabama. Built by Hammermill Paper Company, it began operations in 1966 as a 400 ton-per-day pulp mill. Within two years, it was a leading producer of market pulp, supplying Hammermill's own papermaking facilities and other companies at a rate of 500 tons per day, 25 percent above its expected capacity.

In 1978, Riverdale expanded its pulp producing capacity to 650 tons per day by adding additional pulp digesters and a recovery boiler. In 1983, capacity was increased to 1,100 tons per day with the addition of a second woodyard, brown stock washers, a bleach plant, a second pulp dryer and a turbine generator. The production of paper on site began in 1986, when $255 million was invested to install the No. 15 paper machine. It produces 230 tons of uncoated white paper each year. The expansion also included the addition of a finishing room for two sheeters and a packaging operation, as well as a warehouse.

In 1986, International Paper acquired Hammermill and the Riverdale facility. The mill's largest expansion was completed in 1995, at a cost of $350 million. The major element was the No. 16 machine, the largest, fastest paper machine of its kind in the world. It is capable of producing 360,000 tons of reprographic paper annually and runs at speeds of nearly 50 miles per hour. The expansion also included one of the nation's largest de-inking facilities, capable of producing 400 tons of de-inked, recycled pulp per day, a new gas turbine generator that allows the mill to be energy self-sufficient; and two additional sheeters. The mill produces reprographic paper, offset printing paper, converting papers and market pulp.

RUMFORD FALLS, MAINE PULP AND PAPER MILL

The Rumford Falls, Maine, paper mill was built in 1891 by a group of investors led by Hugh Chisholm, who later served as president of International Paper. It joined 16 other mills to form International Paper in 1898 and became one of the company's leading newsprint mills with a daily output of 100 tons. Rumford added a converting plant in 1901 that produced bag and wrapping paper. Unable to compete with inexpensive Canadian newsprint, the paper mill switched to other grades during the 1920s. It closed in 1936 as a result of the Great Depression, but one of its paper machines was transferred to IP's Moss Point mill in Mississippi, where it remained in operation until 1973.

Rumford Falls mill

SINGLE SERVICE CONTAINERS

Single Service Containers, Inc. was founded in the late 1930s to manufacture Pure-Pak paper milk carton blanks at a plant in Chelsea, Massachusetts, using innovative technology developed by the Ex-Cell-O Corporation of Detroit. After experimenting with several types of carton stock, Single Service Containers selected a bleached kraft grade supplied by International Paper's Springhill, Louisiana, mill, which produced the only grade that performed reliably on the Ex-Cell-O machine. In 1940, Single Service Containers opened a new plant in Philadelphia and closed the Chelsea facility a year later.

IP acquired the company in 1946 as part of a strategic plan to branch out into paperboard converting. Single Service Containers,

Inc. operated as a wholly-owned subsidiary until 1948, when it was renamed IP's Single Service Division. During the next three decades, it grew into a leading milk carton producer with 16 manufacturing plants in all parts of the United States. Innovations developed during these years included the pitcher pour spout, the plastic coated milk carton and gallon cartons. In 1979, the division was renamed the Liquid Packaging Division.

SOUTHERN KRAFT DIVISION

Formally organized in 1941, the Southern Kraft Division was one of International Paper's two major manufacturing divisions prior to 1976.

The Southern Kraft Division evolved out of IP's involvement with kraft paper production in the Southern states in the 1920s. In 1925, IP acquired the Bastrop mill in Louisiana from Richard Cullen, a pioneer of Southern kraft paper production, followed two years later with the Louisiana kraft mill, also in Bastrop. To consolidate its new holdings, IP formed the Southern International Paper Company, with Cullen as president; started new kraft mills at Camden, Arkansas, in 1928 and Mobile, Alabama, in 1929; and acquired the Moss Point, Mississippi, mill in 1928. In 1930, this wholly owned subsidiary was succeeded by the Southern Kraft Corporation, also headed by Cullen. The Southern Kraft Corporation opened mills at Panama City, Florida, in 1931; Georgetown, South Carolina, in 1937; and Springhill, Louisiana, in 1939. It was merged into IP in 1941 and became the Southern Kraft Division, with headquarters in Mobile, Alabama.

The Southern Kraft Division was instrumental to IP's success for years to come. Responsible for the development of kraft pulp and paper, the company's most important products, it developed process and product innovations at its research laboratory in Mobile, Alabama, founded in 1946. It also started new mills at Natchez, Mississippi, in 1950; Pine Bluff, Arkansas, in 1958; Vicksburg, Mississippi, in 1967; and Texarkana, Texas, in 1972. At its peak, the Southern Kraft Division operated 37 paper machines, maintained 12 paper mills and managed the company's vast woodlands in the Southern states.

Along with the Northern Division, the Southern Kraft Division was dissolved in 1976 when IP replaced its geographic organization with product-based business units.

Established by International Paper in 1957, the Southlands Experiment Forest (SEF) became the company's central forestry research facility that developed woodlands management techniques, tree improvements and disease controls.

IP acquired the 16,000-acre Southlands property, a former plantation, as a forestry investment in 1947. Over the next decade, it was managed like most other IP woodlands: a small staff planted seedlings, harvested timber and installed firebreaks. But Southlands differed from other IP forests and indeed most Southern woodlands because its natural flora included all four Southern pine species (longleaf, loblolly, shortleaf and slash). To use this unique environment for forestry research and development, IP turned the property into the Southlands Experiment Forest in 1957. Its mission was to test new forestry methods and techniques in cooperation with university, federal and state researchers and to determine their suitability for commercial development.

SEF's first major research project produced IP's SuperTree™, a selectively bred pine species that grows faster, is more resistant to diseases and insects and yields more fiber than unimproved pine trees. From the late 1950s to 1964, SEF tested and improved the Buschmaster Tractor, an all-purpose piece of equipment used for planting, clearing, earth moving and road maintenance. Milestone programs of the 1960s included the development of techniques to control root rot and improve hardwood regeneration. In 1978, SEF started a soils section that included an analytical laboratory for processing soil and foliage samples. The laboratory later initiated a soil classification-mapping project that mapped 4.2 million acres of IP woodlands from 1980 to 1993, enabling forest managers to improve their harvesting and reforestation plans.

The 1980s brought significant changes when IP improved productivity and technologies throughout the organization. The company closed research centers in Lebanon, Oregon, and Bangor, Maine, and consolidated its forestry research activities at SEF, which became responsible for SuperTree nurseries in Texas, Arkansas, South Carolina and Alabama. Productivity improved under SEF's management, enabling the nurseries to sell a significant amount of seeds and seedlings to outside customers. In 1981, SEF started a biometrics section that developed computer models to determine tree growth patterns and harvesting systems in cooperation with outside researchers. The biometrics section also provided foresters with computer software and training to support forest management in IP woodlands across the country.

During the 1980s and 1990s, SEF's Genetics Section bred new tree selections, conducted progeny tests and designed advanced-generation orchards. It also improved the SuperTree to ensure the availability of sufficient fiber supplies after the turn of the century.

SEF has also played a pioneering role in wildlife management. Its studies of the ecology of the gopher tortoise, an endangered species, showed that the reptile's dwindling numbers resulted not from the bulldozing of its holes, as many had assumed, but rather from the depredation of its nests by raccoons and snakes. The discovery led to better methods of locating and protecting the tortoise's burrows. Similarly, IP's wildlife ecologists at SEF and elsewhere devised new ways to safeguard the habitats of other endangered species, including the redcockaded woodpecker, the Red Hills salamander, and the pine barrens tree frog. These efforts have won praise from environmental groups such as the National Wildlife Federation, the National Audubon Society, and the Nature Conservancy.

SPRAGUE PAPERBOARD MILL, VERSAILLES, CONNECTICUT

The Sprague mill at Versailles, Connecticut was built by the Federal Paper Board Company in 1961 at a cost of $17 million. Operating a single paper machine that was christened Yankee Clipper, it was the world's largest recycled paperboard mill and the last of its kind built in the United States.

Unfortunately, demand for recycled linerboard, its main product, was slack during the 1960s and the mill's poor financial performance brought considerable losses for Federal. A turning point was reached in 1968, when Sprague first produced recycled paperboard for Nabisco Brands' folding carton division. For the next two decades, Nabisco bought the bulk of its paperboard from Sprague. Several improvements increased the mill's daily production capacity from 230 to 600 tons.

During the early 1990s, when recycled paperboard enjoyed strong demand, the mill began supplying a range of customers that produced folding cartons, baseball cards and related products. It operated innovative environmental protection systems and did not use ozone depleting chemicals. In 1996, Federal merged with International Paper, which incorporated Sprague into its paperboard operations.

SPRINGHILL, LOUISIANA PULP AND PAPER MILL

Construction of the Springhill mill started in June 1937 under the supervision of Erling Riis, a senior IP executive. The mill was part of International Paper's effort to produce bleached kraft paper used in milk containers, folding cartons, file folders and tag papers. At the time of completion in 1939, it featured extensive bleached pulp facilities and three paper machines. Among these machines was the first Fourdrinier machine that successfully produced kraft paper from 100 percent bleached pulp for use in Ex-Cell-O Pure-Pak milk cartons. During World War II, Springhill produced V-Board, Overseas Fibre Board and offset map paper. A postwar expansion program added a corrugated container plant, a fourth paper machine that produced cylinder board and a chemical plant operated by Arizona Chemical.

Springhill played an important role in the company's environmental protection development program. In 1946, it installed electrostatic precipitators on its six chemical recovery boilers that conserved saltcake and improved air quality. Building on these and other initiatives, Springhill added odor control equipment and water treatment facilities in the 1970s. The mill pioneered the trademarked Springhill line that included some of IP's most important brand-name products.

The paper mill went into decline in the 1970s and ceased its paper manufacturing operations on February 28, 1979. Other IP operations at Springhill include the container plant, wood products plant, converting and distribution center, and Arizona Chemical facility.

The former paper mill was later the site of the Springhill Habitat Area Restoration Demonstration (SHARD) Project. SHARD, initiated in 1995 in cooperation with The Conservation Fund, has restored the ecological integrity of the mill's wastewater basin through the creation of artificial wetlands.

STRATHMORE PAPER COMPANY

Established in 1892, the Strathmore Paper Company became a market leader in fine writing, printing and artist papers.

Originally named Mittineague Paper Company, Strathmore was founded by Horace Moses, a young papermaker from Ticonderoga, New York, who built a small mill near Springfield, Massachusetts, whose single Fourdrinier machine produced its first sheet of paper on December 15, 1892. The mill's first products included cotton-fiber writing papers, bond grades and ledger papers. In 1893, Moses imported a cylinder machine from Germany and constructed a new mill building in West Springfield to house it. After a trip to the Valley of Strathmore in Great Britain where he saw thistles in bloom, he renamed the organization Strathmore Paper Company and adopted the thistle as its symbol.

The company expanded its mills and specialized in artist papers. In 1896, it pioneered fine paper promotion with the production of a colored sample book that educated customers on the use of Strathmore grades for a variety of printing and advertising purposes. Combined with exceptional product quality, this marketing strategy precipitated Strathmore's rise as one of the nation's leading fine paper manufacturers.

Strathmore acquired or built several facilities during subsequent decades. In 1905, it bought a mill in Woronoco, Massachusetts, followed seven years later by the construction of another mill in the same location. The Great Depression of the 1930s brought major financial hardships, but the company survived these years by introducing new grades, including Strathmore Bond, a 25 percent rag-content paper that later

became its main product. To expand production capacity during the post-World War II boom, Strathmore acquired the Keith Paper Company mill in Turners Falls, Massachusetts, in 1953.

Strathmore was acquired by Hammermill Paper Company in 1961. It added the Millers Falls Paper Company in 1982 and joined International Paper in 1986 when IP acquired Hammermill. Two Strathmore facilities, Woronoco I and Turners Falls, were closed during the early 1990s, and Woronoco II is scheduled to close in 1998. IP continues to manufacture high-quality Strathmore grades at Millers Falls, Massachusetts; Hamilton, Ohio; and Erie, Pennsylvania.

TECHNOLOGY

Either working alone or in partnership with suppliers, International Paper has made significant technological advances that have benefited not only the company, but the pulp and paper industry. Key innovations include kraft linerboard used in corrugated containers and bleached kraft paperboard for use in milk cartons and food packaging. International Paper developed new technologies that became industry standards, including continuous digesters and continuous bleaching, computerized controls, twin wire formers and the extensive use of hardwoods for pulp.

In 1931, IP's Panama City mill was the first to make linerboard from kraft pulp on the Fourdrinier paper machine. Fourdrinier linerboard required 30 percent less fiber for comparable strength than earlier linerboard products made on cylinder machines and ran at 1,500 feet per minute (fpm) vs. 500-600 fpm for the cylinder machines.

In conjunction with American Cyanamid, the company developed V-Board, a packaging board used for shipment of military materiel and food rations during World War II. After the war, IP developed other resin and wax

treatment processes, enabling the company to produce corrugated containers for transporting agricultural products to market. Another important development in the corrugated container field was the commercialization of chemical recovery processes for neutral sulfite semichemical pulping using hardwoods at IP's Georgetown, South Carolina, mill in the late 1940s. The process improved container properties while using the wood resource efficiently.

International Paper also developed major advances in the liquid packaging field. In 1939, it was the first company to use a Fourdrinier machine at its Springhill, Louisiana, mill to produce bleached kraft milk carton stock. This was the first paperboard to perform reliably on the Ex-Cell-O Pure Pak machines, which had been commercialized in 1936 to package milk in paper cartons. In 1960, IP's Pine Bluff, Arkansas, mill became the first to produce polyethylene-coated paperboard for milk cartons. Polyethylene stock cost less, performed better at the dairy and was more acceptable to consumers than its wax-coated predecessor. In 1965, the Pine Bluff mill began producing foil-laminated

Pure-Pak carton, stock which had superior barrier qualities and replaced glass gallon jugs in the packaging of soft drink syrups.

The Erling Riis Research Laboratory (ERRL) in Mobile, Alabama, conducted research and development that enabled the company to obtain all primary patents for the economical use of multi-layer coextrusion coatings of ethylene vinyl alcohol copolymers on bleach board to act as an oxygen barrier. Developed for major packagers of citrus juices, this new technology improved the preservation of juice flavor and extended shelf life. ERRL also developed all extrusion coating technology necessary to permit commercial production of these patented multi-layer coated board structures. Another IP contribution to citrus juice packaging was Spout-Pak®, which joined a plastic fitment to the gable-top carton to provide easy opening and closing of the container, and allow for spill-proof shaking. Originally introduced in 1990, Spout-Pak use was extended to the dairy and aseptic packaging markets in 1996.

Chlorine dioxide bleaching was developed at the Hawkesbury, Ontario, laboratory and mill in the 1940s. This important innovation in hardwood use facilitated the first production of kraft dissolving pulp from hardwood fibers at the Natchez, Mississippi, pulp mill in 1950 as well as the production of Supercell® AO-2, a bleached hardwood market pulp introduced in 1955 which was used successfully as a fiber furnish for lightweight papers. The company pioneered the use of hardwoods for milk carton stock at Pine Bluff. The first production of lightweight white papers from 100 percent hardwood occurred at the Mobile, Alabama, mill in 1957, spurring the wider use of abundant hardwoods for lightweight papers.

The company made several significant contributions to the manufacture of dissolving pulp, which is used in manufacturing products such as rayon, cellophane and acetate. The Hawkesbury laboratory developed technology that permitted the use of hardwood sulfite dissolving pulps and later helped develop the

commercial process at the Natchez mill, which was the first in North America to use the kraft process for dissolving pulp. In 1968, the Natchez mill also developed and commercialized the first kraft dissolving pulp for acetate processes used in the manufacture of acetate, textiles and cigarette filters.

International Paper was also a pioneer in the development of new process chemistry and equipment to manufacture pulp and paper. It was the first commercial user in North America of a continuous digester, initially with a pilot plant in 1950 and on a commercial scale in 1956 at the Camden, Arkansas, mill. Together with Kamyr, IP developed and commercialized in 1958 the "cold blow" which reduced fiber damage during digester discharge. In the 1950s, the company became the first to use the Kamyr diffusion washer, first with a pilot plant at the Camden mill and later with the first

full-scale commercial unit at the Georgetown mill. With its reduced water usage and energy costs, the diffusion washer replaced the drum washer as the industry standard.

In 1936, the Moss Point, Mississippi, mill was the site of the first commercial use of a continuous process to bleach pulp replacing the previous batch process. This installation, which used a Hooker Chemical Company process, also represented the first commercial bleaching of kraft pulp. IP was also the first to install the Kamyr continuous bleaching system at its Springhill, Louisiana, mill in the 1940s.

At the Georgetown mill in 1962, IP adapted IBM equipment in the first application of computers to control paper machine operations. In 1968, Canadian International Paper's Three Rivers, Quebec, newsprint mill became the first commercial user of the vertical twin-wire former.

TEXARKANA, TEXAS PULP AND PAPER MILL

The construction of the Texarkana, Texas, mill in 1969 was part of International Paper's effort to increase its capacity to produce coated bleached board and liquid packaging board. Texarkana was initially equipped with one new machine and one older unit transferred from the Louisiana mill in Bastrop. Production started in 1972 with an annual capacity of 231,000 tons.

Texarkana received a $142 million upgrade during the late 1970s that made it the world's largest bleached packaging board mill. Improvements included a third paper machine, environmental technology and new pulping facilities for the production of Supersoft®, a purified specialty pulp used in disposable diapers.

Another improvement initiative was launched in 1988 to modernize the facility

and improve its cost structure. In addition to a rebuild of the paper machines, the $287 million program involved the installation of an Elemental Chlorine Free pulping system. Completed during the early 1990s, these and other improvements made Texarkana a leading low-cost manufacturer of bleached board and fluff pulp products. Today, the Texarkana mill operates two paper machines.

THILMANY PULP AND PAPER COMPANY, KAUKAUNA, WISCONSIN

A specialty paper manufacturer based in Kaukauna, Wisconsin, the Thilmany Pulp and Paper Company was acquired by International Paper in 1986 as part of IP's acquisition of Hammermill Paper Company.

Thilmany's founder, Oscar Thilmany, was a German immigrant who founded a small groundwood pulpboard mill at Kaukauna in 1883 and named it the Thilmany Pulp and Paper Company in 1889. Initially producing newsprint, the mill soon specialized in lightweight packaging grades and made waxed paper for food products starting in 1898. In

1912, it became a fully integrated mill that combined pulp production at a new sulfate kraft mill—one of the first in the industry—with paper production and conversion. An extensive update of its wax conversion department turned Thilmany into a leading producer of carton liners; wrappers for cut meat, candy and fruit; and embossed printing papers.

During World War I, Thilmany acquired the Wisconsin Tissue Paper Company in Appleton, Wisconsin. The latter was shut down in the 1930s during the Great

Depression, and its two paper machines were transferred to the Kaukauna mill.

A milestone was reached in 1945, when the company completed a research laboratory where scientists developed new coating methods and techniques. Research conducted at the laboratory led to the installation of Thilmany's first polyethylene extruder, producing polyethylene-coated papers, whose markets soared during the postwar era. Thilmany started a coater laminator in 1961 that coated a variety of surfaces with silicone and other resins. Thilmany developed a productive relationship with Akrosil, a Menasha, Wisconsin, based firm that specialized in silicone coating.

In 1969, Thilmany was acquired by the Hammermill Paper Company. A versatile niche market producer, Thilmany performed well during the 1970s, when many mainstream paper companies suffered financial losses. To sharpen its competitive edge, the Kaukauna mill installed a $25 million computerized paper machine in 1976 to produce carbonizing tissue, making Thilmany the leading producer in that market.

Thilmany and Hammermill, its parent company, became part of IP in 1986. Backed by IP, Thilmany built a new plant at Knoxville, Tennessee, that manufactured wax coated products for the thermographics printing industry, poly-extrusion grades and silicone-coated release liners.

A series of investments and equipment upgrades expanded Thilmany's output of pulp, paper and converted products. In 1989, new digesters were installed in Thilmany's pulp mill, increasing production to more than 400 tons of pulp per day. In the midst of a steadily declining carbonizing tissue market, Thilmany's No. 15 paper machine was rebuilt in 1995. The $50 million project enabled the mill to run supercalendered kraft grades for the fast-growing pressure-sensitive market.

In 1998, Thilmany will add a new tandem extruder to its converting department which will be used to laminate Thilmany base papers for a variety of flexible packaging applications.

Thilmany Pulp and Paper mill

THREE RIVERS, QUEBEC PULP AND PAPER MILL

Built by International Paper in 1921, the Three Rivers pulp and paper mill in Quebec was the company's first Canadian newsprint mill. Production started in 1922 with four machines. In 1925, the mill became part of Canadian International Paper, an IP subsidiary. The addition of four Fourdriniers in 1927 made Three Rivers the world's largest newsprint mill with a daily capacity of 700 tons. Over the next 20 years, it increased its daily production capacity to 900 tons.

Three Rivers enhanced its leadership in world newsprint production in 1968, when it installed a vertical twin-wire former to produce offset paper, the first commercial application of this new technology. This new technology was later adopted throughout the newsprint industry.

IP sold the facility as part of the sale of its Canadian holdings in 1981.

TICONDEROGA, NEW YORK PULP AND PAPER MILL

Ticonderoga, New York, is a historic papermaking town where International Paper operated three separate mills.

The first, the Lower Falls mill, was constructed in 1878 and rebuilt three years later after a fire destroyed the original plant. It was owned and operated by the Ticonderoga Pulp & Paper Company, which produced soda pulp and fine papers. A second plant, known to locals as the Island mill, was built by the Lake George Paper Company in 1891 and joined 16 other Northeastern paper mills to form International Paper in 1898. Through much of its history, the Island mill produced newsprint on its three Fourdrinier machines.

IP acquired the Lower Falls mill in 1925 as part of the Riordon acquisition and closed the Island mill in 1929 as part of a strategic plan to phase out newsprint production in the North. The Lower Falls mill produced soda pulp until 1940, then switched to bleached and unbleached pulp made from hardwoods. It also shifted from book papers to more profitable fine grades such as offset and text.

IP's third Ticonderoga mill was built on the shores of nearby Lake Champlain in 1968 to replace the small and outdated Lower Falls facility. The existing No. 7 machine was dismantled and rebuilt at the new mill, which also installed the No. 8 machine featuring a 306-inch wire and a top speed of 2,200 feet per minute.

A leader in air and water protection, the mill consistently met or exceeded some of the nation's most stringent environmental regulations. To limit the emission of odorous gasses and wastewater, Ticonderoga built one of the first oil-fired thermal oxidizers in the American pulp and paper industry and installed a cutting-edge tertiary water treatment system in 1979. The Environmental Protection Agency later used the mill's odor control and water treatment systems to develop standards for the industry as a whole.

In 1981, Ticonderoga launched a five-year project to convert its papermaking process from acid-based technology to the alkaline method, which enhanced product quality. At the end of the decade, it installed one of the world's most advanced folio sheeters in its finishing department. In the 1990s, Ticonderoga's principal products were uncoated white papers such as opaques, offset and reprographics.

TONAWANDA, NEW YORK PULP AND PAPER MILL

Originally built by the Chicago Tribune Company in 1924 to produce magazine grades, the Tonawanda mill was acquired by International Paper in 1931. The mill was equipped with two paper machines. As part of an extensive reconstruction program launched after World War II, Tonawanda improved other production equipment. This enabled both machines to increase their speed from 750 to 1,200 feet per minute. A lack of sufficient orders led to a permanent shutdown in 1976.

VAN BUREN, MAINE KRAFT MILL

In one of International Paper's earliest forays into kraft paper production, the company acquired the small Van Buren, Maine, mill in 1920. For several years, it remained the company's only kraft mill but became obsolete when IP acquired a larger and better equipped mill in Bastrop, Louisiana, in 1925. Van Buren closed down in 1927.

Van Buren mill

VERATEC

Organized in 1987, Veratec was a consolidation of International Paper's nonwoven fabrics business—which had started 20 years earlier with the construction of a plant at Lewisburg, Pennsylvania—and the acquired nonwovens business of the Kendall Company.

As part of a strategic effort to diversify into new product lines, IP organized a formed fabrics division in 1969. One of the first products made at its Lewisburg plant, completed in 1970, was Confil®, a nonwoven substitute for conventional woven fabrics. Confil was widely used by apparel manufacturers in waistbands for trousers, interlinings and interfacings. Over the next several years, the nonwoven fabrics division added a variety of new products, including coverstock used in wallcoverings and baby diapers. In 1987, a plant was built in Green Bay, Wisconsin, to produce fabric softener substrate for Procter & Gamble, the division's largest customer.

International Paper greatly expanded the division in 1987, when it acquired the fiber products division of the Kendall Company, a pioneer of the nonwoven fabrics industry since the 1940s. Kendall manufactured coverstock fabric for diapers, liners for floppy diskettes, bleached cotton for consumer use, and a variety of other products. IP merged its formed fabrics division with the acquired Kendall division to form Veratec.

Headquartered in Walpole, Massachusetts, Veratec manufactures nonwoven disposable products such as diaper components, feminine hygiene products and medical gauzes and bandages. It also makes products such as diskette liners, battery separators and graphic wipes. Veratec operates in niche markets that are less cyclical than the pulp and paper market.

In the latter half of 1997, International Paper reached the decision that selling Veratec will increase opportunities for the business and allow it to become a part of worldwide organization as compared to the regional organization that Veratec was within International Paper. By the end of 1997, International Paper began to seek out buyers for the Veratec division.

Facility Location	Year built/ acquired
Athens, Georgia*	1987
Bethune, South Carolina*	1987
Green Bay, Wisconsin	1987
Griswoldville, Massachusetts*	1987
Lewisburg, Pennsylvania	1969
Liege, Belgium*#	1987
Toronto, Canada*	1987
Walpole, Massachusetts*	1987
Yokohama, Japan*#	1987
San Jose Iturside, Mexico	1996

*acquired

closed

VICKSBURG, MISSISSIPPI PULP AND PAPER MILL

Continuous digester Vicksburg mill

The Vicksburg mill, located in Vicksburg, Mississippi, began producing linerboard in 1967 with a single machine. At the time, the mill's paper machine was the world's largest, producing at its maximum 1,400 tons a day. The machine subsequently received several additions and upgrades, including new headboxes in 1975 and a large dryer section five years later. A modernization program started in 1989 made Vicksburg more efficient and increased production capacity to 1,600 tons a day. In addition to supplying all IP box plants, it sold its product to outside customers east of the Mississippi River and overseas. Located near the large Vicksburg port facilities, the mill shipped some of its linerboard on barges to reduce freight expenditures. Vicksburg focuses on a narrow product mix which includes linerboards such as Euromart® and Pineliner® and supplies a broad range of domestic and international customers.

WEBSTER, MAINE PULP AND PAPER MILL

The Webster mill near Bangor, Maine, was one of International Paper's original 17 mills. Equipped with two paper machines that produced a daily output of 25 tons of newsprint, Webster operated its own ground-wood pulp facilities with seven grinders. When Northeastern newsprint production became unprofitable because of strong Canadian competition, the mill switched to book paper and other specialty grades. Located near a large dam, it installed hydro-electric power generators in 1921 to produce electricity on a commercial scale. IP sold the mill in 1944.

WOODLANDS

Woodlands management, long an integral part of International Paper's operations, provides the raw materials base for the company's papermaking and wood products divisions.

Wood became the paper industry's premier fiber source during the 19th century, when inventors pioneered groundwood and sulfite pulp. America's first wood-based pulp was made at a small mill at Stockton, Massachusetts, in 1867. During subsequent years, many paper mills acquired extensive woodlands to secure a steady supply of this vital raw material. The mills that pooled their resources in 1898 to form International Paper controlled 1.7 million acres of timber-land either outright or under long-term leases. Originally concentrated in upstate New York and northern New England, the company's woodlands later included vast tracts in Canada, where the company leased government-owned Crown lands. By 1921, its holdings had increased to 4.4 million acres.

International Paper delegated woodlands management to four subsidiaries that were responsible for their respective sections and dealings with local logging firms: The Champlain Realty Company in New York, Vermont and New Hampshire; the American Realty Company in Maine; the Miramichi Lumber Company in New Brunswick; and the St. Maurice Lumber Company at Three Rivers, Quebec. In 1908, the Champlain Company started an experimental tree nursery in Vermont with hundreds of thousands of young spruce trees that were later replanted on company-owned woodlands and public lands.

During the 1920s, the company acquired timberlands in the southern United States as well as Canada. In 1925, International Paper gained control of the Riordon Paper Company with 10,000 square miles of woodlands in Quebec that were later inte-grated into Canadian International Paper, a subsidiary. Also in 1925, the company expanded into the Southern states and acquired 440,000 acres of timberland to support its kraft mills.

Southern forests differed from their counterparts in the Northern states and in Canada. Southern forests had a longer growing season and faster-growing species, and most of the land was controlled by private landowners. Furthermore, while Northern loggers usually cut trees during the winter and rafted them downstream to the mills in the spring, the Southern timber har-vest was a year-round operation and involved overland transportation. Combined with the South's relatively flat landscape, these factors sparked the development of industrial, mechanized forestry on a scale that exceeded anything then being conducted in the North.

With extensive holdings in Louisiana, Arkansas, and Mississippi, International Paper played an important role in the devel-opment of industrial forestry. During the 1940s, Earl Porter, manager of woodlands for IP's Southern operations, devised the industry's first mechanical tree planter. Drawn by a tractor, the machine had an annual planting capacity of 375,000 seedlings. Impressed with its performance, equipment manufacturers further developed the tree planter, which was widely used by IP and other forest product companies. This new technology enabled company nurseries and orchards to launch an ambitious refor-estation program in the 1950s that improved forest growth, timber quality and Southern land productivity.

During the late 1950s, Tom Busch, a company forester, invented a mechanical tree harvester that felled a tree, delimbed it, cut trunks to size and loaded the logs onto a truck in one continuous operation. These and other technologies revolutionized forest management and supported IP's papermak-ing operations throughout the South.

The company was also active in other fields. As part of its landowner assistance efforts, many foresters educated private woodlands owners in forest management, enabling them to enhance productivity, reduce fire hazards and control diseases. In the 1950s, the company imported sawmill log debarking technology from Sweden and supported its introduction in American sawmills. The system enabled pulp mills to use lumber manufacturing waste in the form of pulpwood chips.

International Paper initiated research and development programs that further enhanced industrial forestry. In 1957, it established the Southlands Experiment Forest in Bainbridge, Georgia, birthplace of the SuperTree™, a selectively bred pine species that grows taller and is more disease resistant than ordinary trees. As part of the company's Dynamic Forest Program, its nurseries and orchards started a large-scale planting program in 1969 that produced 75 million SuperTrees within the first five years.

In 1980, International Paper reinforced its position as a leader in timberland resource management by establishing the most ambitious forest seedlings nursery program in the history of the South. From 1980 to 1983, the company built and

brought into production three SuperTree nurseries designed and operated to meet foresters' seedling quality, packaging and handling needs.

The company's need for genetically improved seedlings peaked during the 1984-1985 planting season. Faced with new challenges, the company explored external markets for its seeds and seedlings. Its pioneering work in genetics, seedling quality and packaging, combined with the strategic location of its facilities, gave International Paper an opportunity to compete successfully in the marketplace. This position was enhanced with the integration of the Hammermill Paper Company's nursery and orchard facilities in Alabama during the late 1980s.

In 1985, the company transferred 6.3 million acres of woodlands, the bulk of its holdings, to IP Timberlands (IPT), a limited partnership. IPT later created new partner-

ships to transfer large tracts of woodlands located in New York, Pennsylvania, Oregon and Washington. It also acquired one million acres of woodlands from the Federal Paper Board Company following its merger with International Paper in 1996.

In 1994, International Paper took a leadership role in the development of the Sustainable Forestry Initiative (SFI), which was developed by the American Forest & Paper Association to ensure that future generations have abundant forests. SFI is a series of guidelines and principles to ensure the practice of sustainable forestry along with annual reporting requirements for public accountability. International Paper was one of the first to publicly endorse SFI, and is one of the few companies to announce that it will only do business with loggers who are trained in and comply with the initiative.

WOOD PRODUCTS

Long the nation's largest private owner of woodlands, International Paper became a major wood products company in 1956 with the acquisition of the Long-Bell Lumber Company, a large producer of plywood and

hardwood lumber. The acquisition of the Masonite Corporation in 1988 further expanded IP's presence in the wood products sector.

At the time it was acquired, Long-Bell included five large manufacturing centers as well as 18 building materials distribution centers. In the course of the next two decades, when it operated as IP's Long-Bell Division, it built a plywood and lumber center at Chelatchie, Washington, and manufacturing plants at Anderson, Indiana; Atlanta, Georgia; Malvern, Arkansas; Nacogdoches, Texas; and Wiggins, Mississippi. Long-Bell remained profitable during the late 1960s and early 1970s, contributing resources to IP during some of the most difficult years in the company's history.

During a reorganization in 1976, Long-Bell was integrated into IP's new Wood Products Division. In 1979, IP started a $30

million wood products complex at Gurdon, Arkansas, and announced that it would build a $60 million plywood and lumber manufacturing plant at Springhill, Louisiana. Another manufacturing plant opened in New Boston, Texas, in 1981. Disaster struck in 1984 at the Nacogdoches, Texas, plywood plant, which was completely destroyed by fire, causing $32.5 million in damage. IP rebuilt the plant, which produced oriented strand board, a composite wood panel product used interchangeably with plywood in home and industrial construction.

A major addition came in 1996, when IP merged with the Federal Paper Board Company, which operated wood products facilities in the southeastern United States.

Facility	Year opened / acquired
Greenwood, South Carolina #	1972
Malvern, Arkansas •	1968
Slaughter, Texas	1979
Longview, Washington*#	1956
Navasota, Texas*#	1956
Weed, California*•	1956
Quitman, Mississippi*•	1956
Sheridan, Arkansas*•	1956
Vaughn, Oregon*•	1956
Chelatchie, Washington*#	1956
Gardiner, Oregon*•	1956
DeRidder, Louisiana*#	1956
Farmersville, North Carolina#	1960
Joplin, Missouri	1967
Nacogdoches, Texas	1969
Eatonton, Georgia #	1973
Henderson, Texas	1974
Leola, Arkansas	1974
Madison, New Hampshire	1974
Sampit, South Carolina	1975
Coushatta, Louisiana•	1979
Gurdon, Arkansas	1979
Masardis, Maine*•	1979
Whelen Springs, Arkansas	1979
Morton, Mississippi	1980
Mineola, Texas•	1981
New Boston, Texas	1981
Springhill, Louisiana	1981
Pleasant Hill, Missouri•	1984
Maplesville, Alabama*	1986
Wiggins, Mississippi*	1988
Tuscaloosa, Alabama*	1988
Armour, North Carolina*	1996
Augusta, Georgia*	1996
Johnston, South Carolina*	1996
Newberry, South Carolina*	1996
Washington, Mississippi*	1996
Jefferson, Texas	1996

* acquired

• sold

closed

ZANDERS FEINPAPIERE AG GERMANY

Founded in 1829, Zanders is one of Europe's leading producers of high-quality papers. Zanders joined the International Paper family in 1989.

Founder Johann Wilhelm Zanders launched the company on July 28, 1829, when he acquired the Schnabelsmühle in Bergisch-Gladbach in western Germany. Built in the 1580s, the mill had passed through several ownerships and received extensive updates that made it the region's leading manufacturer of handmade paper. The first Fourdrinier was installed in 1860.

Zanders extended its operations when it acquired a nearby paper mill, the Gohrsmühle, in 1868, followed by the Dombach mill in 1876. Two decades later, an extensive reconfiguration program added a box plant, coating machines, railroad connections, storage facilities and power plants. Zanders manufactured coated artist grades, writing papers, envelopes, light printing papers and colored boxes that were considered the leading products of their kind. Unlike American paper mills during the late 19th century, Zanders employed many women in production-line jobs who, like their male counterparts, received a range of progressive benefits such as health insurance and pensions.

In 1930, Germany's economic collapse forced Zanders to close its historic Dombach mill, which had been built in the 17th century, and cut production at its two remaining paper mills. After a short-lived recovery in the mid-1930s, World War II forced the company to reduce papermaking operations and convert some of its facilities into tank repair plants that became a target of Allied bombers.

During the postwar decades, Zanders rebuilt its power plant and straw cell factory, added two paper machines and introduced Chromolux®, a coated paper grade. By the 1970s, the plant operated nine paper machines with an annual output of 115,000 tons of high-grade papers. In 1965, Zanders acquired the Reflex paper mill in Düren, Germany, which produced postal stamp paper and other specialty items.

During the 1980s, a reorganization of its corporate structure turned Zanders into a publicly held company, which launched its first stock offering in 1984. Five years later, members of the Zanders family sold their shares to International Paper.

Following the sale came a large-scale restructuring, including the shutdown of one paper machine and a workforce reduction. In an effort to reinvigorate its manufacturing operations and sales, Zanders implemented the Total Quality Management system and introduced new specialty papers in 1995. The company's American operations, known as Zanders U. S. A., worked closely with IP's Fine Papers Division.

The staff of the International Paper Centennial Project would like to extend its appreciation to the many individuals—especially past and present IP employees — who so graciously contributed their time, artifacts, documents and memories. We have listed below as many of these individuals as possible, and apologize for any inadvertent omissions or misidentifications. Taken as a whole, the artifacts, documents, and memories which we have obtained constitute an unparalleled stockpile of information about the first century of International Paper Company's operations. These materials will serve as a significant resource not only for the company's Centennial, but also for future International Paper anniversaries.

CALLERS TO CENTENNIAL PHONE LINE

Stephen Adams
Jesse Carl Aiken
John Akino
Joan Anderson
Ella Marie Andrews
Guy J. Arnold
Henry Askins
Esther Avant
Edward Bailey
Carl Barkley
Gordon Barnia
Aurore Batson
Rob Beach
Louise Bell
R. S. Belton
Stefan Berger
Jeane Blanchard
Raymond Boeckerman
Darry Bradley
Annette Brandenburg
A. D. Brewer
Blanche Bright
Amiel Brinkley
Donald Britt
Lena Myrabella Brown
Richard Bryant
J. C. Buckley
James Burks
William Burnim
Harry Bush
Myrtle Byrd
Eugene Cannon
J. C. Carter
Donald Clark
Val Clay
H. L. Clinkscales
Bob Collins
Rafael D. Colon
A. Harold Cox
James Creer
Betty Creten
Walter Eugene Crowell
Blanche Crum
Paul Dauget
Pearl Davis
Henry Dellinger
Bonisasio Delmundo
Ishmael Denney
Mildred Diamond
Henry Charles Doherty
Mike Dupont
Richard Durk
Marcia Edwards
Carl Ernst
Jim Evans
Norris Faggard
Binnie Farmer
Thomas K. Finch
Catherine G. Fitzgerald
Jo Ann Ford
Jim Fort
William E. Foutz
Del Frasier
Domenico Frederico
Vera S. Gadberry

Clifford B. Galusha
Elton Garris
Henry Gayles
Marvin Glasgow
Dorothy Grangaard
Dennis D. Gray
Goldie Greer
Charles M. Guthrie
Kinny Haddox
Frederick Keith Hall
Wayne Hall
Thor E. Hare
William Holmes
Robert Houhne
Wilbur J. Houston
Thomas A. Howells
Fred Huey
Lawrence D. Ingram
Merrill Jackson
William A. Johnstone
Chester Jones
Classie Jones
Don Kallio
George Kanouse
Gaylord Karle
Dennis Kearney
Nina Kearney
Katherine Kerkes
Bill Kleinhans
John Kohn
John Kolmetz
Warren Krup
Peter Kuchma
Lawrence J. Kugelman
Lester Kussow
Erna Langseth
Walter Leahy
C. R. Lee
Marie Lenz
Larry Lian
Leo Long
Robert L. Lovelace
Alma Dolores Lundberg
Virgil MacIntosh
Frank Martin
Ruby Mashburn
Angie May
Rossi McCormick
Ellen McLaughlin
Charles McMahon
Mark Middlebusher
Myron Miller
Bharat Mithel
Bea Mitsch
Harold Moore
Dennis Morgan
Willie Morris
Dee Murph
Timmy Neal
Darlene Newman
Antoinette S. Nimsger
Serno Norboe
Darren Nowell
Gary Nyman
Margaret Oliveria
Andre Ouellette
Sophia Palles

Oscar Palmer
Ammaline Parish
Ben Patrick
Thomas Pehl
Anthony S. Pepe
Stanley Pienkowski
Leonard Pierce
Robert Polson
Carl Poston
Al Proto
Delores Reynolds
Sharon Reynolds
Michael Ring
Berlin Rivers
Betty Roberson
Maurice Robinson
Otha Robinson
C. B. Rotton
William Rowe
Josephine Russell
Wally Sabin
William R. Samuels
Vernon Sawyer
Antoinette Sbano
H. G. Scanlan
Joe Scheuber
Lowell Schmidt
Albert Schrock
Peggy Schuh
Wanita Schultz
Terry Secrest
Marvin Seibert
Dallas Sellars
Howard Sinnard
Elizabeth Skerritt
Mary Anne Slocum
Edwin L. Smith
Fred Snell
Ronald Songer
Don Stiling
William Storey
Marvin Sullivan
Mae Summers
Shirley Swiesc
John Tate
Eileen Tesch
Ruanne Thomas
Gerald Thompson
Aaron Thornton
Berlie Tickel
Royal Tidmore
Patricia Tighe
Michael Tobash
James R. Tobermann
Hugh Vanderbilt
Jackie Vaughn
Mitch Vickers
Jewell T. Warren
Carrie L. Washington
David Westerhouse
Frederick J. Wewers
Denise Wiggins
David W. Williams
Charles Wilt
Earline Windham
James Q. Yance
Harriet Yannaci
Julius Zagorski

DONORS OR LENDERS OF ARTIFACTS AND DOCUMENTS

William Aarington
William Abernathy
John Ackerman
Della Allen
Jon Alper
Carlene Anderson
Doug Anderson
Bob Andzulis
Harold Arneson
Jim Baker
Janet Barrineau
Lewis Bartlett
Melanie Baumbach
Gerald Eugene Bean
Thomas Beasley
John Becraft
Ralph Beech
Thomas Berry
Jim Bessant
John Bettis
John F. Birkner
J.B. Black
Lawrence Bledsoe
Jenny Boardman
Bill Boehmler
Fernando Bonilla
Sandra Booth
Richard Boutin
Al Bowerman
William Boyce
Matt Boykin
Wayne Brafford
J.C Breazeale
Julie Brennan
Russel Brenzel
Sherri Brock
Robert Brown
Morty Bruner
Jill Burbary
Robert Burns
Myrtle Byrd
Dixie Callendar
Gerald Canfield
James Carlaw
Geneva Carmouche
Gene Carnathan
Kim Carpenter
Jim Caryer
Linda Casey
Florine Casper
Marie Castiglia
Stephen Cernek
Bill Chuber
Shirley Clarkson
Elizabeth Cobb
Guy Coleman
Robert Connelly
Curtis Connolly
Ernest Cook
Jim Cope
Tom Corley
Pamela Cozzi
Wayne Craft
Brad Crafts
Eleanor Craig
Margaret Craig
Jeff Crawford
Kathy Crawford
Charles C. Cunningham
Brian Dangler
Jay Daniel
Oneal Danner
Hans Peter Daroczi
Ron Davidson
Bertha Davis
Dorothy Davis
Everett Davis
Katherine Davis
Larry Day
W.C. Deal
Clint Dellinger
Mark De Laurence
Gus DeLoach
Thomas Dempsey
Rick Dennis
Lillie DeShields
Bernice Dever
Kendall Dexter

John Dillon
Richard E. Doctor
Kimberly Dogan
Frank Dorsey
Michael Doyle
Armin Dressel
Irvin Dryer
Jennifer Duck
Jack Duddy
Mitch Dudley
Doris Duelley
Valerie Duggen
Eli Duguay
Kenneth Dunlap
Howard Easley
Angela Edwards
Burl Ellzey
Tracy Ewatt
Gretchen Falb
Bert Falley
Phil Farrin
Darwin Fender
Joe Ferguson
Catherine Fitzgerald
Kelly Fitzpatrick
Robert J. Flittner
Brenda Flowers
Laurence Ford
Chester Foster
John Foster
Albert Fournier
Bill Franklin
Bradbury Franklin
J.F. Freeman
Jett Freeman
Reginald Frost
McClellan Gail
Jim Gallion
Norman Gamso
Ralph Gerhart
Bob Gifford
Pamela Gilchrist
Bill Gillis
Dennis Gingles
Mary Alice Gladin
Artie Gohagen
Roy Goodson
Dennis Gorman
Fred C. Gragg
Hugh Gray
Ron Gray
Charlie Greenberg
Jim Guedry
Joe Guttman
Kinny Haddox
Mary Hall
Caryn Hamner
J. Stone Hancock
Thomas Harding
Harold Hardy
Barbara Harper
Brenda Harris
Kathy Harris
Larry Harris
John Harvey
Tom Harvey
David Hatton
Obie Hawley
Helen Hay
Fujio Hayashi
Evans Heath
Gary Heinz
Curtis Helms
Dan Hiers
Sharon Highlander
Hugh Hill
Allen Hillard
Ralph Hinton
Margaret R. Holloway
Amy Hood
Jan Hossack
Bennie Howard
Aaron Howell
Charles Hudnall
Hillary Hufford
A.L. Hughes
Daryl Husovitz
Save Imeson

Bill Irwin
Gary Jackson
Judy Jackson
Myrel Jackson
Mary Jarrell
Jesse Jeffus
Bernard Jennings
Andrea Jentzen
John Jepsen
Alan Johnson
Faye Jones
Joann Jones
Walter Joves
Donald Joye
Howard Judy
Margaret Judy
June Kaczur
Erhard C. Karl
Nina Kearney
Pamela Keaton
Dollie Keckler
Phillip Kemp
Elizabeth Kennedy
Laurance Kenny
Charles Keppler
Linda Kerechek
Patricia Kerner
Stanley Kijowski
Tim Kilfoy
Jimmie Lou King
Richard King
William Kise
Karen Kitzmiller
Charles Klement
Herman Knappe
Peter Kuchma
John Kuhn
Irving Lasky
Dick Lathan
Ruby Lauzon
Don LeClerc
David Leggett
Betty Leslie
Andrew Lessin
Tanya Lewis
Jerry Lindsey
Benjamin Little
Germaine Lorden
Rich Lowe
Joseph Lukowski
Carl Lund
Marty Lundy
Mary Magnussen
Cathy Mann
Edward F. Mannelli
Donald Marks
Lois Markstrom
Bernadette Marosco
Joseph Martino
Charles E. Mason
Shirley Mason
Steve Massey
Roscoe Masterman
J.C. Matlock
Roger Matlock
Mac Matthews
Dick Mattison
Charles Maxam
Robert Mays
John McCall
Vanessa McCants
Kevin McCarthy
Michael McCauley
Frank McCourt
Heather McDonald
Kathleen McGarry
Patrick McGee
John E. McIver
Edward V. McKenna
Hugh McManus
Dan McQueen
Timothy Meade
Jeanie Means
Rajool Mehta
Carolyn Bean Merchant
Norma Merz
Jody Messersmith
Earl Moeller
Joe Montana
Corleen Morris
W.E. Morris

William Morrow
Chip Moser
Lisa Moser
Dottie Mullen
Ernest Murrah
Bob Murray
Ellen Myers
Lynn Myers
Patsy Myrick
John Nakaoka
Charlie Nash
Warren Navis
Roger Nelson
Joan Nies
J.D. Nix
Peter Noyes
Jack O'Brien
Don Ocheltree
Benny Ogburn
Edward O'Keefe
Dave O'Neal
Bobby Ott
Rick Ouellette
Sophia B. Palles
Diane Palmer
Paul Parker
Marianne Parrs
Lonnie Paschall
Shirley Patrick
Lyle Patten
Ron Patterson
Charles Patteson
Sam Pattison
Maureen Paulson
Brad Peters
Elizabeth Pfroener
Robert Pharr
John Phelps
Dick Piepenbring
Gene Pierce
Judy Pirro
Stanley Plimack
Charles Pomeroy
Edward Poole
Helen Poore
Colleen Pope
Linda Price
Vince Prunty
Monica Prusik
Nick A. Pult
Kristen Pushman
Bronson Quickel
Regina Ralph
Daymon Rambin
Ken Ramsey
Phillip Ratajczak
Art Ravenscroft
Bob Rawls
Harold Ray
H.M. ("Minge") Read
James Reed
Bob Reeder
Robert Rhoden
Carol Ribar
Vernet Rice
Kristie Rich
Herschel Richard
Cherri Richards
Patti Richards
Sherry Richardson
Thomas Riddell
Mark Riegen
Cathy Riggs
Cheryl Robbins
Mark Robbins
Michael Roberts
Betty Robertson
Greg Robertson
Jack Robertson
Jay Robertson
Betty Rodgers
David Roland
Rita Roper
Jackie Rosensteel
Cindy Roton
C.B. Rotton
Bob Roush
Walker Rowe
Elwin Rozyskie
Bernard James Russell

Carl Safranski
Yola Salandrea
Sandra Sanders
Dana Saucier
Harold Schmidtgal
Alan Scott
Bob Scott
Joe Scott
Allan Scrafford
Alfredia Seals
Jackie Shaffer
Lavana Sheffield
Angela Shepard
Walter Shorter
Jack Simmons
Bobbie Ann Sims
Robert Singler
Bruce Sinnard
Jill Sistare
Mark Skeesick
Truman Skinner
Charles Slatek
L.C. Sloan
David Smith
Gettis Smith
Mac Smith
Peter Smith
H.T. ("Snuffy")
   Smitherman
Frederick Snell
Charles Snodgrass
Louis Soltis
Albert Sovey
Richard Spitzer
Mark Stanland
George Steimer
Keri Stephany
Herman Stephens
Kathy Steuck
Judy Stevens
John Stiles
Ken Stovall
Richard Strain
Joe J. Strauss
Bill Sullivan
Molly Sullivan
Paul Sundin
John Sutton
Brent Sverdloff
Mary Tabor
Hal Tanner
Frank Taylor
June Taylor
Francis Therrien
Dennis Thomas
Calvin Thompson
Marvin Thompson
Richard Thompson
Russ Titel
Toby Toberman
Peter Tocco
Francis Topper
Russell Trojan
Brian Turcotte
Jack Turner
Carol Tutundgy
Mary Kaye Ulczak
Eleanor Urtel
Karen Valentine
Patricia Van
   Audenhove-Neman
Herb Vando
Doug Varvel
Barbara Vasil
Jesse J. Vaughn
Johnny Vickers
Patricia Villari
Edward Vincent
Larry Vise
Joe Wagner
Alton Wallace
Harold Walters
Bobby Ward
Ronnie Ward
Elizabeth Wasielewski
David Watson
Jules Weiss
Ann Wellborn

Lori Welsh
O'Neal Wheeler
Elaine Wheelus
Diane Whipple
Don White
Susanne White
Colleen Whiting
Art Whitmore
Lisa Wicker
Steve Wieder
Jack Williams
Thomas ("Tweeter")
   Williamson
Bill Wilson
Elaine Wing
Harold S. Winger
Tina Yepes
George Young
John Young
Richard Young
Lucile Youtzy
Judy Zeigler
Mary Zelhofer
Dale Ziegler
Kristin Zschiesche
Tina Zug

ORAL HISTORY INTERVIEWEES

Hildegard Alef
Dempsey Amacker
Michael Amick
Doug Anderson
Bob Arbogast
Robert Armandi
Elizabeth Bailey
James M. Barnes
Roy Barnes
Frank Beal
Gerald Eugene Bean
Franz-Josef Berghausen
Ben Berry
Theresa Bilodeau
David Birch
Lloyd Black
Ray Boivin
Larry Booker
Jesús Bóveda
Al Bowerman
Francis Bowles
Jim Boytin
Matt Boytin
Sarah Boytin
Bill Brabston
Annette Brandenburg
Jean Bridier
Don Brinskele
Clarence Brown
Clyde Brown
John T. Brown
Julie Brown
Kenneth Brown
Larry Brown
Marion Brown
Robert Brown
Ursula Bruck
Hugh Burnham
Isreal Cage
Dever Campbell
Terry Campbell
Linda Casey
Bobby Clark
John Clary
Kirk Clayborn
Charles Connelly
Lysiane Courcimault
Forrest Crabtree
James Craft
Wayne Craft
Brad Crafts
Larry Crammond
Tommy Cruse
Charles Cunningham
John Cureton
Hans Peter Daroczi
Frank Darsey
Carolyn Daugherty
Kenneth Davenport

E.J. Davis
Alan Day
Fritz Dersch
Kendall Dexter
Carl Dickens
John Dillon
Mike Doiron
Richard Doiron
André Dollé
Cecil Dumas
Isaac ("Ike") East
Nancy Eidt
George Ellis
Pat Ellis
Javier C. Espagnol
Binnie Farmer
Phil Farin
Darwin Fender
Mike Fenech
Joe Ferguson
Jorg Fischer
Charlie Fletchinger
Pat Flood
James Foste
Albert Fournier
June Franchetti
Eugene Franklin
Calvin French
Sheila Friedman
Cliff Gaither
Norman Gamso
Edwin Gee
John W. Gilbert
Jim Gilliand
Ferna Girardin
Umberto Giuntoli
Bob Goins
Fred Gragg
Eloise Gravel
Louis Grissom
Louis Gunning
Patrice Hadorn
Sharon Haines
Carlton Hall
John Hall
Shorty Hall
Irma Hammack
Lanus Hammack
Jay Hanchett
Nolan Harper
Aileen Harvey
David Hatton
Fujio Hayashi
Charles Haynes
Ila King Herndon
Billy Hipp
Ric Holland
Theresa Howatt
Benno Hundgeburt
Dexter Jackson
Walter H. ("Shoe
   String") Jackson
Karl-Heinz Janssen
Chappelle Johnson
Joe Johnson
Cathy Joyce
Larry Judd
Erhard C. Karl
Francis Kelly
Charles Kennedy
Benis King
Irving King
Jimmie Lou King
Roy King
Richard Klinger
Fanny Koljonen
Emile H. Kruseman
Mieko Kurihara
Peter Lee
Morton Levy
Joe Lex
Tom Linder
Pierluigi Locchi
Charles A. Logan
Dornell Logan
Douglas Logan
James Logan
Jerome Logan
Preston Logan
Sheila Logan

Terrance Logan
William Logan
Carl Long
Carl Lund
Marty Lundy
Ed Mardosa
Patrick Martin
Victor A. Martinex-
   Angles
Charles Mason
Roger Matlock
Mac Matthews
Kevin McCarthy
Mac McCarthy
Matthew McCarthy
Susan McCarthy
Alvin McDonald
Mac McLean
Carolyn Bean Merchant
Helmut-Josel Mertens
Horst Mewes
Karl Moore
Marty Murphy
Bill Nelson
Roland Neu
Horst Neuhauser
Louis Nuziére
Jeremy M. ("Jerry")
   Oakhill
Victor Oaks
Veronica O'Donnell
David Oskin
Andre Ouellette
Percy Ouellette
Norm Paradis
David Parks
Charles Patteson
John Patteson
T.E. ("Red") Patteson
Thomas Patteson
David Paxton
George Payton
Ken Perkins
Lula Perkins
Gerry Phillips
Richard Phillips
Daniel Ploix
Gilbert Prélade
Devoy Price
Nick A. Pult
Daymon Rambin
H.M. ("Minge") Reed
Adrice Richards
Annette Richards
Bobby Richards
Gilbert Richards
Zeke Richards
J.T. Roberson
Mary Roberson
Bilbo Rodgers
Michael Rodgers
Denise Roush
William F. ("Sandy")
   Sanders
Metha Schlish
Francis Scott
Janice King Scott
George Shamblin
Curtis Silvernail
Neree Simoneau
Jimmy Smith
Wes Smith
H.T. ("Snuffy")
   Smitherman
Albert Soucy
Gert Staiger
Margaret Steele
Joe Strauss
Paul Sundin
Thomas J. Tait
Joseph Trillat
Earl Trimmer
Bert Turmel
Guy Turmel
Jack Turner
John Tyler
John Vandillon

Andrew Vaughan
Melva King Vaughan
Alfredo Verucchi
Augustine Verucchi
Donnie Verucchi
Mark Verucchi
Robert Verucchi
Johnny Vickers
Sybil Vickers
Sam Wadsworth
Chet Walker
Ion Walker
Ken Walsh
Harold Walters
Paul Washburn
Ernest Watson
Lee Weeks
Bill Welch
Calvin Wells
Mary Wells
George White
Lee A. White
Leo Whitstine
Don Whittemore
Janie Wilkerson
Larry Wilkerson
Delbert Williams
Jerry Williams
Page Williamson
Rayford K. Williamson
Thomas ("Tweeter")
   Williamson
Claude Willoughby
Gordon Willoughby
Linwood Wilson
Harold S. Winger
M.L. Wood
Sam Woodham

REVIEW TEAM

John Dillon
Mike Amick
Bob Byrnes
Tom Costello
Doug Fox
Jim Melican
David Oskin
Marianne Parrs
Wes Smith
Milan Turk

Linda Childs
Charlie Connelly
Alan Day
Jim Foster
John Gilbert
Jim Gilliland
Jim Guedry
Fred Gragg
Louis Grissom
Leon Hammond
Chuck Kolodzey
Neal Linkon
Joyce Margulies
Mack Matthews
Bill Michaels
Norm Mjaatvedt
John Nugent
Rick Ouellette
George Payton
Brad Peters
Gene Pierce
Jim Robison
Parker Stevens
Mark Sullivan
Ken Walsh
Rebecca Wix
Sam Woodham

PRODUCTION TEAM

Jenny Boardman
Phil Giaramita
Gene Jones
Karen Kitzmiller
Errol Savoie

Credits:

Researched and written by:
The History Factory
Chantilly, Virginia

Design, concept and development by:
WondriskaRusso
Farmington, Connecticut

Printing:
The Hennegan Company
Florence, Kentucky

Prep:
Scanning: 3900 Linotype-Hell Digital scanner.
Stripping and assembly: Barco.

Presses:
One Heidelberg Speedmaster 8 color
Four Heidelberg Speedmaster 6 color
One Harris 44" x 60" 5 color

This project required:
66 press approvals to print
6,715,000 impressions.
Paper weighed 592,527 pounds.

Paper specifications:
Cover Wrap
80lb Beckett Concept
Cashew text

Flysheets
105/5pt Zanders T-2000 text

Uncoated
100lb Strathmore Renewal
White text

Coated
100lb Zanders Ikono
Dull Satin text

International Paper
Two Manhattanville Road
Purchase, New York 10577
www.internationalpaper.com